Date Due

JUL 07 01			
JUL 10 01			

4/98

Jackson
   County
      Library
         Services

HEADQUARTERS
413 W.Main
Medford, Oregon 97501

To the Young

SCIENTIST

Reflections on Doing and Living Science

ALFRED B. BORTZ

FRANKLIN WATTS
A Division of Grolier Publishing

New York • London • Hong Kong • Sydney
Danbury, Connecticut

For my son, Brian S. Bortz,
and all the young scientists he teaches;
and in memory of Lawrence H. Norris,
who introduced this young scientist to the
wonders of physics.

Photographs ©: Courtesy of Alfred B. Bortz: 8, 11; Bill Branson: 76, 78; Courtesy of Dr. Frank Asaro, Lawrence Berkely Laboratory: 32, 34; Dr. Glen A. Izett: 27, 41; Ernest Orlando Lawrence Berkeley National Laboratory: 29, 30; Kenneth Andreyo, CMU: 105, 109; NASA: 16, 22; Courtesy of the National Institute of Health, Department of Human Services, Genetics Education Office: 62, 64; Peter Arnold Inc.: 101 (Ford Motor Company), 17 (Alex MacLean); Photo Researchers: 55 (Biosystems Technologies/SPL), 50 (Scott Camazine), 74 (CDC/SS), 107 (Alan L. Detrick), 47 (Ken Edward/Biografx); Ramona Boudreau: 13, 14, 20, 25; Courtesy of Richard E. Smalley:, 46, 52, 59; Richard M. Castillo: 97; Courtesy of Richard Morgan, NIH/NCHGR: 71, 72; Courtesy of Roberta Nichols: 95, 99; University Publications: 82, 87.
Illustrations created by George Stewart.
Interior design and electronic pagination by Carole Desnoes.
Map created by Gary Tong.

Library of Congress Cataloging-in-Publication Data

Bortz, Alfred B.
    To the young scientist: reflections on doing and living science / Alfred B. Bortz
    p.   cm. — (to the young . . .)
    Includes index.
    Summary: Well-known scientists from a variety of fields tell how they developed an interest in science, how they got where they are today, and things to think about when considering a career in science.
    ISBN 0-531-11325-6
    1. Scientists—United States—Biography—Juvenile literature. 2. Science—Vocational guidance—Juvenile literature. [1. Scientists—Biography. 2. Science—Vocational guidance. 3. Vocational guidance. 4. Occupations.] I. Title.
    Q141.B744   1997
    509'.2'273—dc20   96-25864
    [B]   CIP
                                                                         AC

Contents

Acknowledgments

Special thanks to Tom Cohn for suggesting the theme and title of this book.

Thanks also to my Internet friends who suggested these interesting interview questions:

- Was there a time when your curiosity led you to cause a problem or to screw something up so badly that a parent or another adult said, "No more experiments for you, kid!"? (Judi Smith, jsmith@bcfreenet.seflin.lib.fl.us)
- Have you ever had an experiment or observation in which almost everything went wrong, something that you might call "the experiment from hell?" (Tina Velgos and daughter, Stefanie, tzvelgos@aztec.asu.edu)
- Do you ever dream about your work? If so, tell us about your most interesting dream. And: Is there a role for the amateur scientist today? If so, what? (Dorcas_Metcalf @brown.edu)
- When you were a teenager, did your peers consider you to be what today's teens would call a nerd? If so, how did you deal with that? (Christine K. Law, lawchri@vetmed. auburn.edu)
- Have you ever felt discouraged about your work, your choices, or the future of your field? If so, describe the areas of discouragement and how you dealt with them. How do you deal with changes in your field? (Georgia Ehlers, gehlers@aruba.ccit.arizona.edu)

Most of all, to the scientists who permitted me to visit and interview them during the summer of 1995, I say: Thank you for believing in this project, and, more importantly, for being an inspiration to the young scientists who will read this book.

Introduction

Personal Reflections on Doing and Living Science

Some students with great self-reliance
Were repairing their teacher's appliance.
They replaced a bad part,
Pushed the switch, heard it start,
And said, "That's what you taught us in science!"

This is a very personal book for young people like you who love, live, and breathe science. Because it is a personal book, it begins with a personal message from me, the author, to you, my readers. Although I do not know most of you personally, I remember when I was just like you. The times may have changed since then, but young people who love science have not.

Writing this book has been, in many ways, a dream come true. I met a number of scientists whose work I had admired for a long time; and I discovered a number of others, previously unknown to me, whose work was equally fascinating and admirable. I am delighted to share that dream, and those meetings, with you.

Since science is so diverse, I tried to cover as many different fields as possible; but since the length of the book must be limited, I naturally focused on research that fascinated me. Because science is a human pursuit, I also made a point of selecting the best human beings I could find. One of them, Indira Nair, is a dear friend and former colleague. Many times I have

Author Fred Bortz ponders a question from a young scientist at West View Elementary School near Pittsburgh, PA.

jokingly told her, "I want to be like you when I grow up." When you read Chapter 7, I hope you will see why.

My friend Indira, and all the other scientists profiled here, are worthy models for all of us. I am not saying that you should strive to be exactly like any one of them. Rather, I am saying that each of them has admirable qualities. By adopting a little bit of each of them, anyone could become a better person.

Because the sampling of scientists in this book is so small and the variety of humanity is so great, it would never be possible to include people of every race and nationality here. So if you don't find someone here with a background like yours, it would be incorrect to assume that there are no scientists who look like you.

In fact, you can be sure there are many scientists who came from families that look like yours. I probably contacted some of them on the way to writing this book, but for reasons of personal preference or schedule, they could not or did not want to be included. The important thing about all the scientists you will meet in these pages, and the thousands of other worthy individuals whom I might have chosen instead, is not that they look like you do, but rather that they *think* like you do.

They also want to share the joys of the scientific life with young scientists like you. They want you to know that you can be both a scientist and a human being at the same time. That's important because, in many ways, you are like other young people. You are interested in other things besides science—perhaps sports or music, art or literature, history or current events. You care about your family and have one or two close and special friends. You may dream about having your own car; you may have or want your own computer.

It is your interest in science that makes you different from some of your peers. You may be fascinated by rocks and minerals and spend hours looking at them. Do you carefully chip away and polish them to understand their properties and to see their beauty? You may study insects. Do you peel away the bark of trees, dig in the mud, crawl on the ground, and turn over stones looking for a rare specimen? Do you enjoy observing their interesting behaviors?

Maybe you seek out dark places where late at night or early in the morning you can see astronomical wonders: a meteor shower, the planet Mercury, a dim and interesting nebula, a comet. If your interests are a bit more practical, you may tinker for hours, taking apart and rebuilding household appliances, motors, machines, or building devices of your own design.

Are you sometimes so persistent and inquisitive about your special interest that you become lost in your thoughts? Do you occasionally wonder where such single-mindedness might take you in life?

If you answered yes to any of those questions, this book is certainly for you. Don't read it in the usual way. Instead, consider your reading a scientific research project and treat the book's pages as a source of data. You have two research questions: "What does it mean to do science and to live a scientific life?" and "What must I do to prepare myself to live such a life?" Each chapter of the book provides you with one or more "research subjects."

Treat each chapter as a set of observations about a scientist or group of scientists working in an interesting area. As you collect your data about the scientific life, remember that the quality of your observations depends on the instrument you use. Since no instrument is flawless, even the best observations are imperfect.

In this case, your observation instrument is a unique combination of software and "wetware" known as Bortz's Brain, which operates inside the skull of yours truly. I am a person, author, scientist, and former college professor who has a particular viewpoint about the scientific life. The "raw data" of these observations come from two sources—my research and my personal interviews with the scientists during the summer of 1995. You do not have access to that raw data; rather you have only the processed data in the form of this book.

As you consider the data that you find here, you may begin to see patterns and to develop theories of what it means to do science and to live a scientific life. You will probably begin to compare those theories to your own life. You may begin to draw inferences about your future, but it is important not to jump to firm conclusions.

Remember that you are a scientist and that your observations are imperfect. Ask yourself: "Where can I find more and better data?" Revisit a chapter to look at it in a new light; seek things you may have overlooked there. Then go beyond this book to other writings about the scientists and their work.

If you are particularly fascinated with certain scientists or their projects, you may consider doing "primary source" research by contacting those scientists yourself. Before you do that, however, you must build a strong base of knowledge about their work and then choose your questions carefully. Most scientists welcome letters from other scientists, especially young ones who have taken the time to understand their work.

If you follow this approach to research, you will probably find yourself awash in observations and details about the scientific life. You will then be prepared to look for patterns in those details and to build theories that relate to your own life. Next, you will ask more questions, which will lead to more observations, more detail, new patterns . . . and on and on you will go.

As a scientist collecting data, you will be trying to assem-

FRED BORTZ

Current field of work: Science writing; Science education

Business title and mailing address: 1312 Foxboro Drive, Monroeville, PA 15146

Date and place of birth: November 20, 1944, Pittsburgh, PA

Education: B.S., M.S., Ph.D. in Physics, Carnegie Mellon University

Significant accomplishments:

- Author of three previous books
    - *Superstuff! Materials that Have Changed Our Lives,* Franklin Watts, 1990, ages 12–up.
    - *Mind Tools: The Science of Artificial Intelligence,* Franklin Watts, 1992, ages 12–up.
    - *Catastrophe! Great Engineering Failure and Success,* Scientific American Books for Young Readers, 1995, ages 9–14 (One of only nine books designated a Selector's Choice on the National Science Teachers Association Children's Book Council list of Outstanding Science Trade Books for Children for 1996).
- Founder, National Forum on Children's Science Books.
- Co-founder, Carnegie Mellon University's summer Careers in Applied Science and Technology (CAST) program for high school students.

Previously worked as: University faculty member in physics and science education; physics researcher; scientific or engineering staff member on projects in nuclear power, automobile engine pollution control, computer systems design, and computer disk systems.

Words of wisdom: Remember that your observations are imperfect. Ask yourself: "Where can I find more and better data?" Revisit your research and look at it in a new light; seek things you may have overlooked.

ble new knowledge, trying to see the big picture in scattered sections of a partially completed jigsaw puzzle, trying to determine the rules of a game by watching people play it. You will be trying to understand.

So prepare yourself to meet a varied and interesting group of scientists. Most of all, enjoy your research!

Chapter One

Carolyn and Eugene Shoemaker: Preparing for the Unexpected

While exploring the Meteor Crater,
He imagined a Moon trip years later;
But the heavenly sights
And the comet-filled nights
Were his wife's, and their fame's growing greater.

When Carolyn Shoemaker found her first comet in 1983, she had just begun to think of herself as a scientist. She never dreamed that a dozen years later she would hold the record among living comet hunters (thirty-two as of June 1995) and would be closing in on the all-time record of nineteenth-century astronomer Jean-Louis Pons—thirty-seven. She also never dreamed that her work would bring her worldwide fame and acclaim a decade later.

On March 25, 1993, Carolyn Shoemaker was peering into the dual eyepieces of a stereomicroscope, studying three-dimensional views of the sky created from the film from the previous night's telescopic photography. It was tedious work; she took out pair after pair of negatives, carefully aligning them in her viewer, and painstakingly examining the images. Most of the time she saw nothing but familiar stars, planets, nebulae, and other heavenly bodies—beautiful, yes, but well-known to her after more than a decade of searching the sky.

Still, she searched patiently, hoping to find something unusual. Sometimes in the midst of such routine work, her mind

Carolyn Shoemaker (right) has discovered more comets than any living person and is second only to a nineteenth-century French astronomer overall. Her record is largely due to her skill with and major contributions to the techniques of using a stereomicroscope, like the one shown here, to examine three-dimensional views of telescopic images of the night sky. Her husband, geologist Eugene Shoemaker (left), is a frequent collaborator in her work, just as she is a frequent collaborator in his.

would drift to the day a dozen or so years earlier, when, already past her fiftieth birthday, she first got into the business of seeking the unexpected.

When I was a youngster, I was interested in the skies— I think most youngsters are. I was interested in the stars and I would look at the moon and think, "I wonder what's beyond it." But my feelings didn't go any further than that. I didn't really know any scientists, and as I grew up, perhaps more typically than Gene [her husband Eugene Shoemaker], I did not know what I wanted to do.

I found many subjects interesting, but I didn't find them compelling. It was not until our children were grown and had left home that I turned to science, and that was really incidental. I wanted something to do besides volunteer

CAROLYN SHOEMAKER

Current field of work: Planetary Astronomy

Business title and mailing address: Lowell Observatory, Mars Hill Road, 1400 West, Flagstaff, AZ 86001

Date and place of birth: June 24, 1929, Gallup, NM

Education: Chico State College, Chico, CA, B.A., 1949, M.A., 1950

Significant accomplishments:

- Developed efficient stereoscopic techniques that have more than doubled the rate of sky coverage of a major telescope at the Palomar observatory.
- Discovered more than 800 asteroids, including 44 that are approaching Earth.
- Discovered 32 comets including Shoemaker-Levy 9, which was in orbit around Jupiter and impacted the planet in July 1994.
- Investigated meteorite craters and ancient impact sites in Australia in collaboration with Eugene Shoemaker; discovered and collected many notable meteorites.
- Several prestigous awards and lectureships, including an honorary Doctorate of Science.

Previously worked as: Teacher, community volunteer.

Words of wisdom: The opportunities in science are both for men and women—equally. Neither a young man nor a young woman should hold back because of gender. . . . But to be successful in it, you have to give it your full attention. You have to have it as a burning desire. . .

work. I turned to Gene . . . and said, "What can I do now? Have you any ideas?"

And he said, "I have this little program in searching for asteroids and comets"—mostly asteroids at that time— "and maybe you'd like to work in it."

And so I said, "Let me try it out." I still didn't have any strong feeling for it, but I really was still looking for something like Gene [had] . . . work that was also his hobby, his primary interest. I wanted something just as absorbing.

So I thought I would try it, and I just gradually slid into astronomy by the back door. . . . I hadn't taken courses in astronomy; it was a constant learning curve for me, and I began to get very excited about it. I discovered I could go to the telescope and have lots of fun just taking the films that we used.

I discovered that examining the films was equally interesting, perhaps even more fun for me, because we had developed a stereomicroscope, and it was a technique that enabled me to look at things in three dimensions. More and more I discovered that I could spend not only all day, but I could spend half the night, and I could spend most of my waking hours [looking at the images]. In fact, if the day had 48 hours in it, I could easily spend 48 hours just working on asteroids and comets.

And the more I worked, the more I thought about it, and the more I learned, and the more I read. So it has been—even until this day—a learning process. You need to keep learning all your life.

If you're lucky, and you know what you want to do [when you're young], that's great; but it doesn't mean that you cannot start at any particular time later in your life. I was really lucky, too, to have someone like Gene who had [developed] a pretty good background in conveying information, and who was also a believer in girls and women learning and doing things. [He] was an enormous encouragement to me always.

If her mind had been drifting, the image in front of her eyes brought her quickly back to business. She called to her husband, Gene, and their friend, writer and amateur astronomer David Levy, who were working nearby.

Look at this, she told them. They stared at an image unlike anything any astronomer had ever seen, an image of the object that came to be known as Comet Shoemaker-Levy 9. A little over a year later that comet brought them sudden and unexpected fame when it crashed into Jupiter with spectacular results. Carolyn Shoemaker describes the discovery:

This particular comet was exciting later on, but it was [also] exciting at the time I found it because it was so unusual looking. Most comets are round with a coma [a halo of atmosphere] and many times with a tail. . . . But this comet was shaped like a bar. It looked like someone had stepped on a round comet and flattened it. It also had a coma and tail, but it was very strange. We knew we had something exciting and different when we discovered it.

We learned three things about this comet. The first was that it was fragmented, and no one had ever seen a comet completely fragmented into so many pieces as this one was. The second discovery was that it was in orbit about Jupiter, and no one had ever seen a comet while it was in orbit about any planet. [Author's note: That explained the fragmentation. "Tidal" forces caused by Jupiter's gravity pulled

Comet Shoemaker-Levy 9, as photographed by the Hubble Space Telescope on July 1, 1993, more than a year before its dramatic collision with Jupiter. Says Carolyn Shoemaker: "We knew we had something exciting and different when we discovered it."

the comet apart into a "string of beads" when its previous orbit brought it very close to the giant planet.]

The third discovery came on May 22. The discovery that it was going to impact Jupiter was a fabulous thing to us. At that time, I was a little dismayed because I knew I was going to lose a comet, and I get to feeling very personal about all comets. Gene was excited because he had always dreamed that he might possibly see an impact. He wasn't thinking in terms of other planets; he was thinking in terms of our Earth. But we were fortunate that this [one hit] another planet.

Gene Shoemaker's dream of being "on the scene" of an impact began early in his career. As a young geologist in the mid-1950s, he explored Meteor Crater, a famous meteorite impact site not many miles from his present home in Flagstaff, Arizona. Most scientists at that time believed that the huge crater—more than 0.8 kilometers (0.5 mi.) in diameter and nearly 150 meters (500 ft.) deep—resulted from the impact of a huge meteor in fairly recent geologic time (perhaps about 10,000 years ago). Some, however, had other theories. According to one of these theories, the crater was volcanic in origin.

The scientific disagreement is important. There are many sites with older craters and craterlike structures in the world. Because these other sites are so much older, they have undergone physical and chemical changes, such as erosion. As a result, it has been difficult to determine their origins.

Gene Shoemaker set out to find a way to recognize even very ancient impact sites. As a good scientist usually does, he put himself on the track to discovery when he asked himself some important questions: "What kind of evidence might a meteorite have left here in the rocks at Meteor Crater? Would the same kind of evidence survive millions of years at other impact sites?"

As he thought about the moment of impact, he realized that the rocks at an impact site would be subjected to enormous temperatures and pressures, far beyond those that are found in volcanoes. He knew that laboratory studies of rocks

Eugene Shoemaker's research into the crystal structure of minerals found at Meteor Crater, Arizona, in the 1950s provided conclusive evidence that it was indeed caused by the impact of a iron-rich rock from space.

under great heat and high pressure produced chemical changes and new crystal structures, yielding minerals unlike any observed in nature up to that time.

If such minerals existed, they would survive for millions of years as the "signature" of a meteoric impact. So Gene Shoemaker decided to look for high-pressure minerals in the rocks at Meteor Crater, where they ought to be relatively easy to find. Although he takes great pride in the discovery, he describes it modestly.

> We've been very lucky to have had a lot of surprising discoveries. One very early in my career was the discovery of very high-pressure minerals at Meteor Crater, Arizona. I guessed that they might be there, and we went and looked. Sure enough, there were minerals with crystalline structures that had only been produced in the laboratory under very high pressures. These minerals then gave us a "fingerprint" with which we could identify other impact sites on the Earth.

Unlike his wife, Gene Shoemaker has always known he wanted to be a scientist. In fact, he has always been a scientist.

His work at Meteor Crater can be traced back to his childhood fascination with rocks.

Like many other children, when I was small, I liked to pick up rocks. In fact, I became completely fascinated with them; and in the small town of Torrington, Wyoming, where I spent the summers with my father, the streets were paved with pebbles from the North Platte River. They were beautiful pebbles in my eye, and I would spend hours and hours smashing them open to see what they looked like on the inside.

Very soon that led to systematic collection of minerals and, later, of fossils. So I simply fell in love with rocks and minerals and fossils at a very early age, not knowing then, of course, that one could actually make a lifetime profession out of such an interest.

By the time I started high school, I knew that it was possible to make a living as a professional geologist and aimed directly towards that. So I was very lucky to know at an early age precisely what I wanted to do. . . .

By the time I graduated from college, I had a game plan. It was about a 10-year game plan. In fact, most of that game plan came to pass. I was lucky enough to be able to make it happen. I've sort of had a rolling 10-year game plan for the rest of my life.

Gene Shoemaker's long-range game plan as he explored Meteor Crater included dreams of embarking on a much more exciting expedition—a journey to the moon. Had that part of his game plan come to pass, he would have achieved public fame much sooner than 1994, and he would have known well in advance that it was coming. It's clear, however, to hear him describe it, that he was seeking not fame but rather knowledge and adventure.

I had a personal ambition as a young man. I had the idea long before there was a NASA, long before there was a space program, that human beings would actually get to the

Eugene Shoemaker (right) founded the field of astrogeology. He is particularly interested in impact events within the solar system. His wife, astronomer Carolyn Shoemaker (left), enjoys sharing his work and has collected several significant meteorites on their joint expeditions to possible impact sites around the world.

moon in the course of my lifetime. And I imagined that the principal reason in going to the moon would be to study the geology. Why else would you go? That's the main science that one does on the moon.

So I had this game plan to try to be . . . the first geologist to go to the moon. In fact, that game plan was coming along pretty well until the very last moment. It was cut off by a failure of my adrenal cortex, which simply disqualified me medically from being an astronaut.

However, I did have the satisfaction that one of the younger men who had worked with me at the time, among five who applied to be scientist-astronauts, did become a member of the astronaut corps, and he did go to the moon to study the geology, and that was [Harrison H.] "Jack" Schmitt. So I had the great satisfaction that one of the people that I helped bring into the field did go and do those things I would have liked to have done myself.

Science is often described as an almost inhumanly pure, precise, exact, and logical field. However, listening to Eugene Shoemaker talk about his lost dream of going to the moon, and listening to Carolyn Shoemaker speak of the fun she has while working at the telescope and of the dismay she felt at the prospect of losing "her" comet, you realize the importance of human traits in scientific progress.

For instance, if Gene Shoemaker had not been so adventuresome and ambitious as to prepare himself for a trip to the moon as a young man, would he have been motivated to spend the rest of his career developing the important new field of astrogeology? His description of that field may suggest an answer.

Astrogeology is my favorite subject because it is a field that I essentially helped define. It's a cross-disciplinary science that involves aspects of both geology and astronomy. One is studying the geology of the planets using the tools of the astronomer but the basic approach of the geologist. It consists of working out in detail the structure and the sequence of deposits that formed on the planetary surface and deducing from that the history of the planet—the planetary evolution.

A big part of that history, it turns out, on the planets of the inner solar system has involved the bombardment of those planets by smaller interplanetary bodies: comets and

Eugene Shoemaker had hoped to see the farside of the moon from a space capsule, but he had to settle for photographic views such as the one taken on the Apollo 11 mission.

asteroids. So as we look out to our own moon and to Mercury, and Venus, and Mars, we see those surfaces peppered with the results of that bombardment—with impact craters—which is a big part of that story. Another part of that story has been to work out the rate at which those craters were formed so we could put a time frame on the actual planetary histories.

In later years, as we sent spacecraft out deeper into the solar system, the Voyager spacecraft in particular, we then got images of the moons of the more distant planets. Each one of those turns out to have its own history recorded on its surface and, in most cases, a detailed history again of that bombardment of smaller interplanetary bodies.

So the science involves both the careful understanding of the bombardment, . . . reconstructing the geological history and interpreting those events not just for the physical history, but also for what they might mean for the evolution of life here on Earth—and possibly life in other places. One of the places I think we should be looking, for example, is the global ocean under the global ice pack of the satellite Europa, one of the large satellites of Jupiter. If we're going to discover life in the solar system, that's where I would go next.

The most important human trait for success, in science or any other field, according to Gene Shoemaker, is the willingness to keep on with the work.

Above all, the most important ingredient in success in any career, especially in science, is dedication. It's persistence. It's ongoing, long-term persistence that finally leads you to achieve large things in science.

Carolyn Shoemaker agrees, but adds:

There's another factor which is very important in science: a curiosity to discover everything and anything that there is to learn about an area, and to examine what you discover with an open mind. It's very easy to have a preset idea of what you should be seeing or finding, but it's the open mind and curiosity that leads you on to discover other things.

Eugene and Carolyn Shoemaker's hard work individually and jointly, together with their unfailing curiosity and open-mindedness, have prepared them for the unexpected throughout their lives: never-before-seen minerals at Meteor Crater, an unexpected career as a comet-hunter, a comet shaped like no other ever seen, and sudden fame as the world watches fragments of that comet smash into Jupiter.

Even though they were not expecting to become celebrities, their approach to science and to life prepared them to accept their sudden fame and to turn it to beneficial ends. Carolyn Shoemaker describes it best:

> My feeling was one of utter amazement and surprise, sort of like "Who are they talking about? It couldn't be me," and then an awareness that I really should respond to this interest in what we have done.
>
> It's been a real period of growth for me personally, just learning to respond to people . . . to convey the real excitement that I feel in the search for these bodies.

The Shoemakers' celebrity has given them a rare opportunity to share the excitement of their work with the general public. Their message to young people considering scientific careers goes beyond that. They see both opportunities and difficulties ahead. Technology and scientific knowledge are continuing to expand rapidly, but jobs for scientists are not.

Gene Shoemaker puts it this way:

> There's only one reason to ever think seriously about pursuing a career, or more precisely a life, in science, and that is because you deeply want to do it. . . . Opportunities [today] are limited. They're there, but the only people who will succeed are the ones who are absolutely dedicated to doing it.

Carolyn Shoemaker adds a woman's perspective:

> The opportunities in science are both for men and women—equally. And neither a young man nor a young woman should hold back because of gender. This is sometimes a problem for women because we have not always been trained to think as scientists. . . .

EUGENE SHOEMAKER

Current field of work: Astrogeology

Business title and mailing address: Lowell Observatory, Mars Hill Road, 1400 West, Flagstaff, AZ 86001

Date and place of birth: April 28, 1928, Los Angeles, CA

Education: California Institute of Technology, B.S., 1947, M.S., 1948; Princeton University, M.A., 1954, Ph.D., 1960

Significant accomplishments:

- Discovered coesite (a high-pressure form of silica) at Meteor Crater, Arizona. This finding firmly established that the crater was created by an impact and was not volcanic.
- Investigated structure and history of the moon, established a lunar geological time scale, developed methods for geological mapping of the moon.
- Established and developed the field of astrogeology.
- Led several major projects for the National Aeronautics and Space Administration (NASA). Many of these projects involved geological study of the moon and other bodies in the solar system.
- Recipient of nearly twenty major awards, medals, and honorary doctorates including the National Medal of Science, which was presented by the president of the United States in a White House ceremony.

Previously worked as: Nothing else. He was a geologist from childhood.

Words of wisdom: The most important ingredient in success in any career, especially in science, is dedication. It's persistence. It's ongoing, long-term persistence that finally leads you to achieve large things in science.

Science is very rewarding. I find myself wondering that I never considered that as a career when I was a youngster. But to be successful in it, you do have to give it your full attention, and you have to have it as a burning desire these days. But it is not something that should be overlooked when you consider what your future holds.

Chapter Two

Frank Asaro and Helen Michel: What Killed the Dinosaurs?

When the asteroid struck with a blast,
It created a dust cloud so vast
That the skies rained iridium.
Now the dinos, we pity 'em,
For it made them a thing of the past.

When Nobel Prize-winning physicist Dr. Luis Alvarez and his geologist son, Dr. Walter Alvarez, brought some unusual Italian limestone containing distinctive clay deposits to chemists Frank Asaro and Helen Michel in 1977, none of them imagined that the clay held the secret of what wiped out the dinosaurs—and the majority of other living species—65 million years ago. Yet 3 years later when they first published their findings and interpretations of an *iridium* layer in that clay, scientists all over the world took notice.

The article stated that the clay contained unusually large quantities of the element iridium. The cause of that excess, they wrote, was that 65 million years ago, an asteroid approximately 10 kilometers (6 mi.) across collided with our planet. The impact created a global dust cloud that obscured the sun for many months or years. The lack of sunlight and the consequent changes in climate led to the extinction of many species of plants, the animals that fed on those plants, the animals that fed on those animals, and so on up the food chain to the dinosaurs.

CLEAR CREEK NORTH SITE, COLO.

Coal

Impact layer

Claystone

Carb. shale

TERTIARY

CRETACEOUS

Evidence of the impact of an asteroid at the Cretaceous-Tertiary boundary can be found in rock samples from all around the world. The thin layer of clay in this carbon-rich piece of polished rock from the Clear Creek North site south of Trinidad, Colorado, contains an unusually high concentation of iridium and grains of shocked quartz, both hallmarks of the impact. The team of Luis Alvarez, Walter Alvarez, Frank Asaro, and Helen Michel first found evidence of the event in a clay layer in piece of limestone from Gubbio, Italy.

Their idea was, on one hand, a bit outrageous; but it was also fascinating. Asaro recalls scientists' reactions to it.

When it was published in *Science*, it received a great deal of comment. The most important statements to us were made by [famous paleontologist and best-selling author] Stephen Jay Gould, and he said that it doesn't matter if it's right or wrong. What's important is that it's testable.

This is what had a tremendous appeal to the scientific community. It could be tested, and it could be tested in

many different disciplines—a lot of work, many people—
and this was appreciated.

After more than a decade of research, most scientists now accept the once bizarre idea of Alvarez, Alvarez, Asaro, and Michel. In fact, there is strong evidence that the impact site has been identified.

The story of that research is also the story of how scientific theories develop. It illustrates how new ideas spring up at the fringes of science, how most are quickly discredited through systematic attempts to test them, and how those that survive may ultimately become part of the core knowledge. In parallel to that story runs the account of how two unlikely young people came to be chemists, colleagues, and authors of a scientific paper that captured the attention of the entire scientific community.

Why call Helen Michel and Frank Asaro "unlikely?" In Michel's case it was simply that she was a woman growing up in the 1940s. She recalls:

> When I was in high school, I took chemistry and I found it absolutely fascinating. I loved the laboratory work. After graduation, I talked with a number of friends whose fathers were either in chemical engineering or some engineering science. I was exploring what sort of jobs women could have in chemistry, and every one of them advised me to become a nurse. . . . I guess I was a little stubborn, because I totally ignored them and started taking chemistry. . . . I thought, well, I didn't know what was available at the end of the line, but it was a good way to go through school at least.

After trying to get a job in chemistry, Michel decided to come back to the University of California at Berkeley for graduate school. Asaro, who worked at the Lawrence Berkeley Laboratory, adjacent to the University, hired her as an assistant, and they have worked as colleagues ever since.

As for Asaro himself, he grew up in a working-class environment. Most people then assumed incorrectly, as many still do today, that young people from such homes should never have great dreams. Asaro's story proves them wrong.

> The most important thing in my family was a love of education, or at least the need for education. My mother was very proud of her eight grades. My father made it to second grade. I will add that when he was 65 years old, he graduated from high school.

Helen Michel's careful, painstaking work in nuclear chemistry had led to a number of important research papers even before she and Frank Asaro discovered high concentrations of iridum in a piece of Italian limestone brought to them by Nobel-Prize winning physicist Luis Alvarez and his son, geology professor Walter Alvarez.

H E L E N   M I C H E L

Current field of work: Orchid breeding

Retired from: Analytical Chemistry, March 19, 1990

Mailing address: Orchids Orinda, 1330 Isabel Avenue, Livermore, CA 94550-9239

Education: B.S., 1955, University of California, Berkeley, graduate studies at University of Indiana

Significant accomplishments:

- Was responsible for major chemical operations, including the handling of radioactive materials, for world-famous nuclear chemistry group at the University of California, Berkeley.

- Collaborated extensively with Frank Asaro and others on application of high-precision methods of neutron activation analysis. In that work, she and her colleagues:

  –determined sites at which important specimens of ancient pottery were made, thereby providing a new archaeological understanding of Middle Bronze Age civilization.

  –exposed the hoax of the "Plate of Brass," supposedly left by Sir Francis Drake but actually made in the late nineteenth or early twentieth century (Michel was lead author on the most notable publications).

  –identified "iridium anomalies" in geological samples from the Cretaceous-Tertiary boundary, from which scientists were able to develop a new understanding of the cause of mass extinctions on Earth.

- Was president of Orchid Digest Corporation and the Orchid Society of California. Has judged orchid shows in the Philippines, Japan, and Costa Rica. Regularly judges orchid displays throughout the United States.

Words of wisdom: You can follow a path which you think is right, but if you don't look back and see where you could have gone wrong, you get into trouble at the end of the line. So you have to very critically look at your work and determine whether or not you have made mistakes as you go.

I saw my parents working very hard. My father was a barber and I knew his feet got awfully tired. . . . He worked long hours, even Saturdays. In those days, women did not work like they do now, but my mother did. She worked in a packing house. Her wrists would hurt; I remember she used to wrap her wrists with bandages to help. Sometimes I would help keep house.

When I went to high school, my parents, to impress me with what was important since I knew how hard they worked for money, gave me half a day's pay for every "A" on my report card. I realized that my father's job was to be a barber and cut hair, my mother's was to be a packer and pack lettuce, and I was to study and go to college.

Michel, like Asaro, works hard, and they also share other traits that have led them to success, most especially their meticulous attention to detail, their constant criticism of their own work, and their understanding of the human capacity for making mistakes. Michel says,

You can follow a path which you think is right, but if you don't look back and see where you could have gone wrong, you get in trouble at the end of the line. So you have to very critically look at your work and determine whether or not you have made mistakes as you go.

Asaro adds,

We realize that we do make many mistakes and we spend a great deal of time correcting them. We are very concerned with the errors in our measurements. If we can keep the errors reasonably small, the [numbers] will take care of themselves.

Their painstaking approach and capacity for hard work enabled Asaro and Michel to become leaders in the use of a technique known as *neutron activation analysis*. This technique enables chemists to detect very small concentrations of elements in their samples.

In neutron activation analysis, the scientists put their sample in a beam of *neutrons*. The *nucleus* of an atom in the sam-

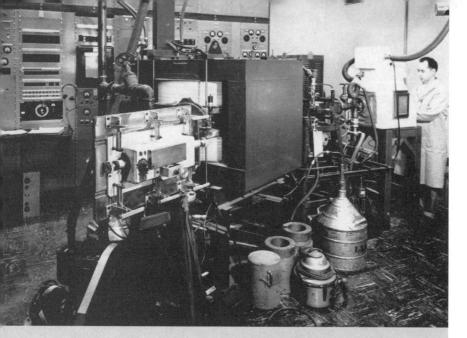

Frank Asaro and the neutron-activation analysis apparatus that he used to analyze a wide variety of interesting samples. This apparatus revealed an unusually high concentration of iridium in a clay layer in a piece of Italian limestone. That result pointed him and his colleagues Helen Michel, Luis Alvarez, and Walter Alvarez to the theory that an asteroid or comet impact caused the mass extinction that occurred at the Cretaceous-Tertiary boundary 65 million years ago.

ple may capture a neutron and become radioactive. After a time, the atom gives off a *gamma ray*. If 1,000 nuclei capture neutrons, then approximately 500 of them will give off a gamma ray in a period of time known as their *half-life*. In the next half-life, approximately 250 more nuclei give off their gamma rays, in the next half-life 125 more emit gamma rays, and so on.

In neutron activation analysis, scientists use radiation detectors to measure the number and energies of the gamma rays given off by a sample. They can use this information to determine what kinds of nuclei emitted the gamma rays. Since a half-life in this technique may be hours in length, measurements often require days of diligent gamma-ray counting.

Since certain kinds of nuclei are more likely to capture neutrons than others, the gamma-ray counts are not a direct measure of the atomic concentrations (or proportions of each different kind of atom) in the sample. To turn counts into concentrations, the scientists need to know how likely it is for the nucleus of a particular element to capture a passing neutron. That likelihood, which can be very large for one type of nucleus and very small for another, is expressed in units called *barns*, which measure the "nuclear cross section," or how large the target nucleus appears to be to a passing neutron. If a particular nucleus, such as iridium, has a large cross section, then it is possible to detect minuscule amounts of it using this technique.

By the 1970s, Asaro and Michel had built considerable reputations for the application of neutron activation analysis to many interesting problems. Asaro was part of a group that compared the composition of the stone in some giant Egyptian statues to stone from various quarries. Their research revealed where the stone had come from and other interesting tidbits of its history. Asaro and Michel together investigated a famous engraved "Plate of Brass," supposedly left by Sir Francis Drake in his 1579 California expedition and discovered in 1936. The techniques of the 1970s, including neutron activation analysis, demonstrated conclusively that the brass could not have been made until the twentieth century.

Their work on the Plate of Brass caught Luis Alvarez's attention. He appreciated Asaro and Michel for their skill, their careful work, and their willingness to apply their most sophisticated techniques to unusual problems. So he and son Walter took their Italian limestone to Asaro and Michel.

The story of what happened next is best told in Helen Michel's and Frank Asaro's own words:

Michel: Walter had brought back a piece of this layer and given it to his father, showing him the two limestone layers and sandwiched in between was the clay layer.
Asaro: Luis thought they could tell how long it took to deposit that layer.

FRANK ASARO

Current field of work: Analytical Chemistry, specializing in neutron activation analysis

Business title and mailing address: Senior Scientist Emeritus, B70-MS195, Lawrence Berkeley National Laboratory, University of California, 1 Cyclotron Road, Berkeley, CA 94720

Date and place of birth: July 13, 1927, San Diego, CA

Education: B.S., 1949, Ph.D., 1953, University of California at Berkeley

Significant accomplishments:

- Developed high-precision methods of neutron activation analysis, and applied them in many areas. For example, he and his colleagues:
  - determined sites at which important specimens of ancient pottery were made, thereby providing a new archaeological understanding of Middle Bronze Age civilization.
  - clarified the history of a number of ancient Egyptian statues by determining where the stone was quarried and revealing repair work on one major statue.
  - exposed the hoax of the "Plate of Brass," supposedly left by Sir Francis Drake but actually made in the late nineteenth or early twentieth century.
  - identified "iridium anomalies" in geological samples from the Cretaceous-Tertiary boundary, from which they developed a new understanding of the cause of mass extinctions on Earth.
- Published many scientific articles in archaeology, paleontology, and geology, as well as in analytical chemistry.

Work since retirement: Retired on September 30, 1991, but "still works full-time (and often more) just for the fun of it."

Words of wisdom: (1) Set your goals very high, so high that you aren't likely to achieve them. (2) There are always opportunities. . . . If one thing doesn't work, try another, and keep on trying another. (3) Don't indulge in risky things very often . . . but once in a while, it's important to take a great risk.

Michel: In the Cretaceous layer below, you could see the little foraminifera (the shells of the animals that lived in that ocean) and they died out very abruptly at the *K-T boundary*, and the new ones appeared later. Luis also knew that large animals like dinosaurs and many other species died out at that time. He wanted to get a handle on how long it was before life returned again.

Asaro: Luis thought that inasmuch as there was a constant rain of cosmic particles upon the earth, that if they could measure the amount of cosmic debris in this 1-centimeter [0.3-inch] clay layer, that they could tell how long it took to deposit.

Luis looked through the literature and decided that the best way to measure the cosmic debris would be the amount of platinum group metals, and in particular one of three elements—iridium, osmium, and rhodium.

Now the reason for measuring the platinum group elements, and these three in particular, is that when Earth was molten about 4.5 billion years ago and the iron went to the core, it carried many elements along with it, particularly iridium. . . .

So when the iron went to the core, it took the iridium from the crust, depleting the crust by a factor of 10,000 compared to the solar system average. In many asteroids or comets or meteorites, you would expect to find the solar system average of iridium. In meteorites, it is about half a part-per-billion. . . .

Luis then looked into the way of measuring these three elements and decided you could get the best sensitivity with iridium, because it has such a large probability of capturing neutrons when any of these come around the atom. It has a 1,000 barn cross section and a barn is a large unit.

So Luis had worked all this out when he came to see us. He wanted to measure specifically the element iridium. He asked me if we could do it, and I said, "No. We've already tried to measure this element in work with a geologist from the U.S. Geological Survey. . . . He did chemical separation on the material [to increase the concentration of iridium] and I still couldn't see it. I did the very best thing that I could do to enhance the possibility of detecting iridium, and we didn't. I don't think it's very likely."

The Alvarezes were extremely charming and persuasive. They [thought that] we could easily dissolve away the limestone, [leaving only the clay] and thus enhance the iridium abundance, which I didn't think very likely [to succeed]. I finally agreed to do the project for three reasons. One, I had a new, [more sensitive] detector, which I was trying to use for environmental work. . . . Second, Luis Alvarez had done some work in looking for holes or unseen chambers in Egyptian pyramids using cosmic rays. I'd been very impressed by the work, and I thought it would be nice to work with Luis Alvarez.

The third [reason] was perhaps the most important. I had been trying to impress geologists with the usefulness of neutron activation analysis—when it's done with high precision and accuracy—to their field. I thought that even if we don't find anything interesting about iridium, we will have these other elements that would be useful to Walter Alvarez.

So I agreed to do the work, but there was no funding and I had a backlog of several months to catch up on. So although we held our discussion in roughly October of 1977, it was not until June of 1978 that we were able to get samples irradiated and start to measure them.

I didn't detect anything in the whole rock sample. Then [using the new detector], we looked at the samples in which we had dissolved away the calcium carbonate. We did see iridium. We saw so much iridium that it could not have been due to the normal cosmic infall. The experiment was therefore a failure.

When Asaro used the word "failure," he spoke with as much care and seriousness as he devotes to his neutron activation measurements; but somewhere behind his intent eyes must have been a little twinkle. The "failed" experiment was the beginning of the biggest success of his and Michel's professional lifetimes.

Still, Asaro and Michel were right to suspect the measurement, since it showed an amount of iridium that would normally take 500,000 years to accumulate from cosmic rays. That time period did not match other measurements of the geologic history of the limestone. Geologists were certain that the limestone layers on both sides of the clay were deposited during the same period in which Earth's magnetic field was reversed from its present direction. They knew the clay—and thus the iridium—was deposited in, at most, a few thousand years.

Scientists always strive to have reproducible results, so they rarely settle for a single measurement. That is especially important when the result is as unexpected and surprising as Asaro and Michel's measurement of the iridium in Walter Alvarez's clay. As good scientists always do, they looked for a simple explanation first.

> **Asaro:** The simplest explanation would be that [the high measured concentration of iridium] was an experimental error. We measured additional samples later on and found [the same thing], so it was not an experimental error.
>
> Luis and Walter decided that the best explanation was that the iridium had extra-terrestrial origin. The reason for this is that you can have local deposits of iridium [with concentrations] quite high compared to what we observed. But we observed the iridium concentration in this 1-centimeter [0.3-in.] layer of clay, and it was thought that this clay was distributed in many different places in the world.
>
> So they considered it to be worldwide in its distribution. [A few months later at a scientific conference,] we published an abstract [or a brief summary of results] that stated we had found iridium, that we thought it was distributed worldwide, and we thought it had an extraterrestrial cause.
>
> We knew that there were thoughts about a supernova

having caused the massive extinctions of life that occurred 65 million years ago. About 75 percent of all genera [or groups of related species] living at that time went extinct. How rapidly they went extinct we don't know, but it was an unusually large proportion. Therefore there was considerable interest in this particular time period, and it had been hypothesized that a nearby supernova was responsible.

So we checked into whether a nearby supernova could have deposited the iridium. We worked very hard at this—some 30-hour stretches. We would work at night and during the day, and we would write up our work in our notebooks. Luis Alvarez would come in the next day while we were sleeping, and he would leave us notes.

Helen and I survived on a potent brand of chili that the machines sell in the laboratory. [We ate that] to keep us awake. [Sometimes], while we were working at night, Luis and Walter would come in with their wives. [They would bring]

Asaro and Michel together: Cookies and ice cream to keep us going.

Asaro: After what appeared to be initial success in correlating our data with a supernova in two different ways, we repeated the measurement much more intensively than at first. We found there was no correlation—that a supernova was *not* responsible for the iridium, and we published that in another abstract.

We looked [more closely at the supernova theory] and decided that it was very improbable that a supernova would have caused this. We looked at the probability that another star would be that close and would go supernova. [That probability was so small that] it just didn't seem reasonable, so we decided that we were now going to deal with high probability events.

Dr. Asaro's modesty is showing here. According to Luis Alvarez' colleague Richard Muller, the Alvarez group was on the verge of publishing that a supernova had been the cause of the extinctions. In his book, *Nemesis: the Death Star*, Muller explains that Alvarez believed that a supernova was responsible because testing showed that the rock sample contained plutonium as well as iridium.

Asaro and Michel's characteristic attention to detail saved Alvarez from potential embarrassment. Their careful checking showed that a bottle of acid used in the chemical processing of the first rock sample had previously been used in an area where plutonium was present. They realized that the acid could have picked up a minuscule amount of plutonium at that site. When they replaced that acid with a fresh bottle and tested a larger rock sample, no plutonium was present.

Luis Alvarez then spent 6 weeks checking through various geological-astronomical scenarios. He would come up with an idea and everybody would hack away at it. Mostly we would decide it was no good and go to another.

He came up with one or two ideas per week . . . one good one or maybe not so good each week. Then he came up with the asteroid impact hypothesis, and there wasn't anything that we could do to shake it or that he could do to shake it. He was doing most of the shaking himself and then would check with a lot of people and couldn't find anything wrong with it.

In this hypothesis, 65 million years ago, a 10-kilometer (6 mi.) asteroid, or possibly a comet, struck the Earth. In doing so, it would have caused a tremendous explosion, equivalent in energy to that of 10 million hydrogen bombs going off at the same time in the same place. This material would go up into the stratosphere—the upper parts of the atmosphere—circle around Earth, and shut off sunlight to the surface of Earth. The plants would die, and the animals that ate the plants would die, and the animals that ate those animals would die, and so on up the food chain.

In January 1980, Luis gave a talk in San Francisco at a meeting of the American Association for the Advancement of Science. [He reported that] we had found the iridium anomaly [not only in Italy but also] in Denmark—but there were complaints from reviewers that Italy and Denmark aren't that far apart from each other.

Well, when Luis gave the talk, there was a gentleman there, by the name of Dale Russell, who had collected samples from New Zealand. We saw his rock, and it looked very much like the Italian rock did, and we saw big holes in it where he had taken samples. We got together [for] dinner after the talk and agreed to work together.

He gave us some of his samples; we found iridium, and we added New Zealand to the paper. New Zealand is as far away as you can get from Denmark and still be on the Earth. So we felt that we had shown it was distributed worldwide. . . .

After our paper was published [in June 1980], people began to test it out in various ways. We ourselves began a very large program of testing. . . . I laid out some ground rules. If we were right, we would have to find iridium at every place where this 65-million-year-old Cretaceous-Tertiary boundary was intact. Where it had been deposited and hadn't been washed away, then we should find iridium there.

We and others went into a massive program to investigate such sites. Over the years, over a hundred such locations have been found, and we have studied about half of them ourselves. In every place where the boundary was intact, iridium was found.

[An important question remained:] Was it truly of extraterrestrial origin? One [indication of] that was platinum group ratios. Things can happen to elements when they weather on the surface of Earth, so you check to see if the ratios are consistent with what you expect from solar system averages that you see in meteorites. The mantle, for example, will have about the same [ratios] as in meteorites, but it's got to get from the mantle to the surface of Earth, and in that process it can change.

When we made very careful checks, we and some others

This magnified, polarized-light image of a grain of quartz from the Madrid site west of Trinidad, Colorado shows two prominent sets of parallel crystal planes. This type of crystal has only been seen in rocks subjected to high levels of shock, such as those resulting from meteoric impacts and nuclear explosions.

found that you could get *exactly* what you would expect from extraterrestrial material. . . .

One of the later experiments that was terribly important was the discovery by the United States Geological Survey of *shocked quartz*. . . . [Author's note: This is one of the minerals that Eugene Shoemaker looks for in his search for meteoric impact sites, as described in the preceding chapter.] As of this time, the only places I know of that you can get [shocked quartz] are in impact [sites] of extraterrestrial material . . or in the Cretaceous-Tertiary boundary. This was confirmation.

There were many other things that confirmed it. One of the biggest uncertainties was the [location of the impact]. . . . Now the crater might not exist because the floor of the ocean is constantly being *subducted* under the continents. Of the ocean floor that existed 65 million years ago, roughly half of it has been subducted.

So it could have been lost. Fortunately it was not. A few years ago [1991], a crater was identified, a buried crater on the tip of the Yucatán Peninsula. The estimated diameter is 180 kilometers [110 mi.]—some estimate it a bit larger. That's the diameter we had projected from the data on the size of the asteroid. The age of melt rock from the crater has been dated. It was found to be the same age, within [100,000] years, as glass associated with the deposits that have the iridium elsewhere in the world.

The distribution of iridium in rocks is markedly different in the area around the crater than it is in other parts of the world. There are huge disturbances that you see on the ocean bottom, and the iridium is concentrated in the top, in the fine layers.

It appears as if there were giant disturbances in the ocean. Huge waves washed out onto the land, almost removing the water from the Gulf of Mexico, and then they came back with a roar and a great force and deposited wood fragments in the sediment on the bottom of what was the ocean then. The wave [went] back and forth in the Gulf of Mexico, depositing sand when it was turbulent. When the wave [went] past, it would deposit the finer particles, the clay, including the iridium.

Michel: A group in Chicago found a lot of soot in that boundary layer from the massive firestorm that came after the impact. [Author's note: that soot contains "buckyballs," an interesting, recently discovered molecular form of carbon, which is the subject of the next chapter.]

Now that the impact site has been found, is the story of the Cretaceous-Tertiary extinction fully told, or nearly so? Not in the least. A wealth of new questions have emerged, and Michel and Asaro plan to apply neutron activation analysis and other chemical techniques to investigate some of them.

Michel: The whole impact on the life sciences—what makes certain things go extinct, how certain things survive—seems to me very much still a good question. Why did the turtles survive and some of the fishes die out?

Asaro: The opportunities for research now are very high. Sixty-five million years ago, there was an impact, and sediments were deposited in large amounts over a very short space of time: minutes, hours, days. With the impact and the initial wave that scoured the ocean bottom, you have a clock starting. As you measure the sediments that are deposited, you have time elapsing.

You can measure time after the impact with considerable precision, considering this happened 65 million years ago. Imagine being able to look at a period extending over a few hours in rock 65 million years old.

These are the opportunities now. You can study the sediments as a function of distance away from the crater. You can see very large amounts being deposited close to the crater. As you move farther and farther away, they get smaller and smaller.

When you're in the western part of the United States, you will see deposits on the order of a centimeter. In places close to the crater, you see deposits that are tens of meters. You see such large deposits that you think they have to represent underwater avalanches.

There is a tremendous opportunity for study. You have a large depletion of life at that time, and here's a place to see how life commences when there's a big depletion. It's known, for example, that things changed immediately. But the Cretaceous species didn't all die out at once. Some of them went out immediately; some of them managed to hang on for a while, but they couldn't compete in the new environment because the rules all changed with the impact.

There was so little activity that some scientists have called it a "Strangelove" Ocean, a dead ocean. Seventy thousand years or so after the impact, that's when the enormous Tertiary bloom started.

What does this story mean to readers like you? Every scientist dreams of playing a part in a major discovery—something that changes the world or the way people think. Asaro and Michel have had the opportunity to live that dream. But as their lives illustrate, you can't go out seeking that dream. Instead, you must first work diligently to prepare yourself for success. Then you must be fortunate enough to have an opportunity for great discovery cross your path. Finally, and most importantly, you must recognize the opportunity when it finds you, and make the most of it.

Frank Asaro, as is his way, describes this process in detail and with great precision:

> Set your goals very high. They should be so high that you aren't likely to achieve them.
>
> There are always opportunities if you keep looking. . . . If one thing doesn't work, try another, and keep on trying another. . . . Many times in looking for the iridium *anomaly*, I'd find it in the last sample. What would have happened if I hadn't run the last sample?
>
> It's very important to look for opportunities, and don't be afraid to take advantage of them. You don't want to indulge in risky things very often, because the probabilities will catch up with you; but once in a while, it's important to take a great risk. I took a great one, and it paid off for me, when I left a good job to come back and try graduate work [although I had come] close to failure in college.

Helen Michel, as is her way, summarizes her approach to life and science with a broader statement: "Be yourself, and don't give up." Without doubt, she and her long-time colleague Dr. Asaro still have many successes ahead of them.

Chapter Three

Richard Smalley and His Bucky-Stuff

As a buckminsterfullerene maker,
He's a molecule-building ground breaker.
Yet in high school, his record
Was certainly checkered.
Now he's truly a "mover and shaker."

For most successful scientists, the discovery that science was their future came very early in life, perhaps as early as the first day that they asked their parents or teachers, "Why?" For others, like Rice University Chemistry Professor and Nobel Laureate Richard E. Smalley, that self-discovery came much later. As he recalls:

> I don't think that most people thought I would amount to anything when I was a high-schooler. Neither did I, frankly. . . . I never thought I would even get a job, let alone be a scientist, let alone [be] lucky enough to have been in areas that have had an impact so far beyond my expectations.

Yet the signs of his future scientific career were present as early as the day his grade school teacher first told him about *atoms* and *molecules*. As Smalley reflects on that day, he naturally jumps forward to his favorite topic: building molecules from clusters of atoms, especially carbon atoms.

Richard E. Smalley's work in cluster chemistry lead to the first discovery of the soccer-ball shaped molecule of carbon that he and his colleagues named buckminsterfullerene.
In 1996, Smalley received the Nobel Prize in chemistry for his work.

I remember in grade school sitting at my desk and hearing for the first time that matter was made up of atoms. I remember looking at the wood of my desk and saying, "Oh, come on! You're kidding me! You mean that way down there are really these little atoms that have this crazy behavior? I don't believe it."

Then increasingly as I heard about this, the more intrigued I became. [I wondered] "How is it that you can possibly be so certain of what's happening down there? It must be just a story that somebody thunk (*sic*) up, and it's a good story, but we really don't know that much about it."

In fact, it is just a story; but we know an incredible amount about it. [It's] an incredible achievement of humankind, of our civilization, to have learned about this. We've learned that the *elements*—the things the world is made of—are composed of atoms, which are incredibly tiny and [which] link together in particular ways.

Some of those, particularly carbon, link together in ways that are very much like balls and sticks, what we used to call Tinkertoys. . . . Imagine balls with little holes in them and you can [connect them] with a few sticks. You can start building structures in a three-dimensional world that are kind of like little buildings.

What I have always been fascinated with—and it increasingly is fascinating not just to me but to a very broad frontier of science—is to really get right down and explicitly build buildings with atoms.

Imagining that you can create tiny Tinkertoy-like structures from atoms opened up a whole new area of science and

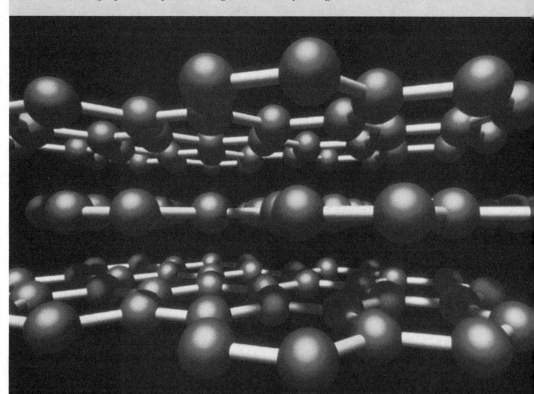

Carbon atoms link together in many arrangements like balls and sticks. Each arrangement has very different properties. In soft, slippery graphite, they are arranged in sheets of hexagons.

technology for Dr. Smalley. He began to think about making structures as small as ten atoms on a side. He calls this the nanoscopic scale because those structures would be a nanometer (one-billionth of a meter) in size. How would such structures behave physically and chemically? What technological wonders could be created? Can you make a box or a tube out of one kind of atom and trap atoms of another kind inside? As you will see, questions like these still drive his research today.

Before Smalley could build buildings with atoms, he and his colleagues had to design equipment that would force the atoms he chose to bond together to form clusters.

> We built [atomic cluster-making] apparatuses of increasing complexity and sophistication so we could figure out where all the atoms are, why they were stuck together, and how tightly they're stuck together. [We built our apparatus] to explore this as a scientific question, not with any particular ax in mind to grind.
>
> It happened that this instrument we built turned out to be a very new kind of "microscope," such that if you put carbon in this microscope and you kind of tweak the lenses to bring it in focus, Bingo! Out pops at you [evidence] that there's something very special about the sixtieth cluster of carbon.

Dr. Smalley is using the terms "microscope" and "lenses" figuratively here. He is speaking of an instrument that enables the scientist to detect very small things ("microscope") and of adjustable components of that instrument ("lenses"). In this case, his instrument is used for cluster chemistry, the study of chemical reactions in small groups of atoms.

> We discovered that [as you cool] carbon vapor with the atoms wandering around randomly at very high temperatures, [the atoms] spontaneously come together to form this object [consisting of sixty carbon atoms]. Sixty is such a large number. You think that, well, if sixty is special, then

probably fifty-nine's not bad, and fifty-eight, and sixty-one, and sixty-two. But uh-uh; just nothin', then sixty, then nothin' again. It's almost as though the apparatus reached out with its hand and grabbed us and said, "I'll bet you can't figure me out!" That was really stunning.

Almost as surprising to Dr. Smalley's group as the experimental result—that sixty carbon atoms come together to form a very special molecule—was how quickly they were able to figure out the shape of that molecule. They simply used their knowledge of solid geometry and out popped the answer.

They take the structure of a soccer ball where every carbon is identical to every other one. What is amazing is that's the only possible answer. Just from [mathematical] inspection, there is no other arrangement of sixty atoms that is an explanation for that one piece of data. . . .

No one had ever predicted that [experimental result] previously. In fact, even now we're involved in major discussions about just how it happens that sixty atoms come together to form this most symmetrical object.

Because Smalley and his collaborators (most notably his Rice University colleague Robert F. Curl and Professor Harold W. Kroto of the University of Sussex in Britain) were the first to discover this symmetrical object, they were entitled to name it. They did so in 1985 when they published their first paper on the subject in the prestigious British journal *Nature*. They realized that the molecule's patterns of hexagons and pentagons were similar to those used in geodesic dome structures of the famous architect R. Buckminster Fuller. In tribute to Fuller, and adding a touch of whimsy to prevent them from becoming too self-important, they named the new C_{60} molecule "buckminsterfullerene."

Within a few weeks, Smalley and his colleagues discovered several variations on the round C_{60} soccer ball. The more elongated molecules, C_{70} and C_{84}, which resembled rugby balls,

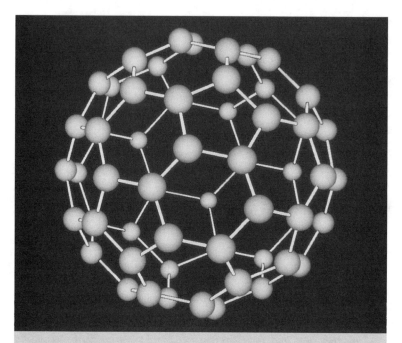

This computer-generated image of the molecular structure of a buckminsterfullerene shows that it is made up of sixty carbon atoms in a pattern of hexagons and pentagons.

proved to be stable, as did several other larger "fullerenes." The newly discovered group of molecules soon acquired a collective nickname, "buckyballs."

The history of buckyball science has a number of interesting twists, not the least of which was that, though completely new to them and most other scientists, these molecules had been predicted by and searched for by scientists in a few other laboratories. Furthermore, the buckyball shape had been studied mathematically for centuries. Smalley describes that history:

> Certainly, we were not the first to think about this structure—the truncated icosahedron. This, to the extent

that one can uncover it in history, was first thought of by Archimedes. So it's over 2,000 years old.

The thought that you could build a molecule with this structure out of carbon had occurred to a person named David Jones in the 1960s. The thought that the particular molecule might be stable . . . had occurred to a Japanese scientist, Eiji Osawa, in the early 1970s.

The thought of trying to systematically build it—synthesize it—in a chemical reaction in normal organic chemistry had occurred to Orville Chapman at UCLA in the late 1970s, early 1980s. He actually had a National Science Foundation grant to build this molecule. . . . Nobody thought he could do it, and in fact, he didn't do it and he hasn't done it yet.

Now we didn't know anything about this. . . . We did not set out to make it. What I set out to do in the late 1970s and early 1980s was build a machine that would allow us to make aggregates—clusters of anything in the periodic table.

Still, although Smalley's group had succeeded in making buckyballs, they could only make them in very tiny quantities. Buckyball science did not really take off until 1990. Once again, it was the result of a chance discovery by two research groups, one German and one American, who were trying to make, of all things, stardust.

For many years, the two groups (led by Wolfgang Krätschmer of the Max Planck Institute for Nuclear Physics and Donald Huffman of the University of Arizona) had been interested in the absorption of light in the ultrathin dust clouds between the stars. Because they could not collect real stardust, they decided to try to simulate it.

They knew that much of the interstellar dust was carbon, so in 1983 they built electrodes from graphite, a common form of carbon, and modified an arc-welding torch to create conditions similar to those that existed when stardust was created. That resulted in a sooty material, which they collected and

RICHARD E. SMALLEY

Current field of work: Cluster Chemistry, especially buckminsterfullerene and related molecules

Business title and mailing address: Department of Chemistry, Rice University, P. O. Box 1892, Mail Station 100, Houston, TX 77251

Date and place of birth: June 6, 1943, Akron, OH

Education: B.S., University of Michigan, 1965; Ph.D., Princeton University, 1973

Significant accomplishments:

- Pioneered supersonic beam laser spectroscopy, one of the most powerful techniques in chemical physics.

- Discovered and characterized buckminsterfullerene and related molecules, and continues to be a world leader in this research area.

- Director of the Center for Nanoscale Science and Technology at Rice University.

- Member of the National Academy of Science and the American Academy of Arts and Sciences.

- Recipient of honorary doctorates from the University of Liège (Belgium) and the University of Chicago, plus several prestigious awards and medals in chemistry and physics, including the 1996 Nobel Prize in chemistry, the 1991 Irving Langmuir Prize in Chemical Physics, the 1992 American Institute of Physics International Prize for New Materials (with R. F. Curl and H. W. Kroto), the 1992 E. O. Lawrence Award of the U.S. Department of Energy, the 1993 William H. Nichols Medal of the American Chemical Society, and the 1995 Franklin Medal.

Previously worked as: Research chemist for a petroleum company

Words of wisdom: When you're still in high school, you're still very much in the process of becoming. Even when I was in my twenties—even in my thirties—I had not really begun to understand what it is like to be Rick Smalley. So when you're fifteen or so, give yourself a break. You don't have to solve all these problems today.

studied. They measured the way the simulated stardust absorbed light, and plotted this information on a graph. The horizontal axis of that graph showed the wavelength of light, a

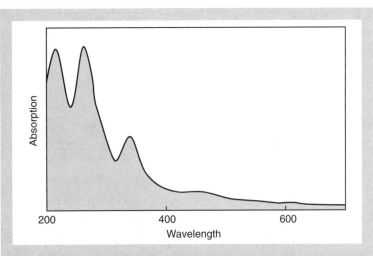

In 1983, German and American researchers trying to make simulated stardust noticed an unusual two-peaked region on the light-absorbtion graph of the material they created. After learning about buckyballs, they thought that their strange result might indicate the presence of buckminsterfullerenes. After considerable work to reproduce "the camel," they announced a new technique for making large quantities of buckyballs.

number related to its color, and the vertical axis described how much of that wavelength is absorbed as it passes through the stardust sample.

The resulting graph had a curious feature, which the scientists named the "the camel." At two wavelengths, which were fairly close together, the absorption of light was notably higher than at other nearby wavelengths. Thus, the resulting absorption spectrum had two small but prominent humps.

"The camel" remained nothing more than a curiosity until the *Nature* article about fullerenes appeared. Krätschmer and Huffman then wondered if the two spectral blips might be due to C_{60} in their stardust. They tried to reproduce the earlier result but had difficulty doing so reliably, so they set their two-humped spectrum aside. Finally, in 1989, they thought about a different way to make and study their sophisticated soot. This time, they succeeded in reproducing "the camel." The following May (1990), they confirmed that they had made buckyballs in large quantities.

It was no longer necessary to use Smalley's complicated cluster chemistry techniques to make mere micrograms of fullerenes. Now people could make grams of buckyballs using nothing more complex or expensive than modified arc-welding equipment.

Suddenly, buckyball science was on a roll. Scientists could now make and study materials based on buckyballs or crystals of buckyballs (buckyballs in a regular three-dimensional arrangement). Some discovered ways to put metal atoms inside buckyballs; others created bucky-crystals with atoms in the spaces between the fullerene molecules. These new materials often would have remarkable electrical, magnetic, or mechanical properties. Krätschmer and Huffman's chance discovery had unleashed a flood of interesting basic research and resulted in pursuit of dozens of potential technological applications. The activity in fullerenes was so great and so fascinating that *Science* magazine, probably the most prestigious scientific journal published in the United States, named buckminsterfullerene "Molecule of the Year" in its December 20, 1991 issue.

Reflecting on the past and looking toward the future of fullerene science and technology during the summer of 1995, Smalley was as enthusiastic as ever.

> It is now 10 years after we discovered that carbon spontaneously forms this molecule. . . . It's been 5 years since [they have] been available in bulk. . . . It's been 3 years since it was discovered that one can make bucky-tubes, tubular extensions of [buckyballs that look like] chicken wire wrapped around to make a cylinder. . . . [It's been] about 3½ years since it's been discovered that when buckyballs are mixed with metals, they can become super-conductors.
>
> Something like 5,000 papers have been published in

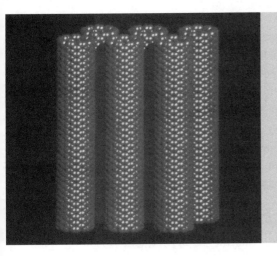

Although, as Smalley says, "Bucky still hasn't got a job," these carbon microtubules, or buckytubes, may have many practical applications.

this area, but still there is not a single commercial use of fullerenes. . . . They're still very much objects of research. We like to say that Bucky still hasn't got a job; he's still in school. This period of time is longer than most of us thought it would take.

To some extent, it's been a slow learner. This kid shouldn't be living with his parents anymore; he should be out there with his own job. So some degree of caution is called for in making statements about big-time applications. On the other hand, this ain't (*sic*) any old molecule. This is a molecule built out of carbon. Carbon is by far—big time by far—more versatile in its chemical bonding than any other element in the periodic table.

Carbon's versatility in forming chemical bonds results, among other things, in the ability to form sheetlike arrays of hexagons with carbon atoms at each vertex (corner) of each hexagon. The resulting structure looks a lot like chicken wire. Just like chicken wire, these carbon sheets can be curled into tubes to form nanoscopic pipes. If you cut out one side of a few of the hexagons and pull the remaining sides together to form pentagons, the result is a ball.

The big picture is not just buckyballs. It's really this: [These carbon sheets can be used as] a building material. . . . If it's just hexagons, it's flat. It's kind of easy to wrap it [into a tube]. And if you extend the tube out, you've got a stick. . . . Or you can [add pentagons] to make a buckyball or larger geodesic dome. Depending on where you put the pentagons, you can get it kind of oblong. You can put domes within domes within domes. [By adding pentagons, you can wrap the one-dimensional sheet] over any structure you can imagine.

Let's imagine that you tried to make a glove for my hand with just one layer of atoms. I'd use just hexagons like this to go along the side. To go along the length of my finger, I'd make a tube. . . . When I get to the tip of my finger, I'm going to have to put in pentagons. . . to give that curvature. . . . But what'll I do about this little part in here [between the fingers]? That's a different kind of curvature. . . . Pentagons don't work down there, but heptagons do—seven-membered rings. It turns out that the cost of putting a seven-membered ring into the sheet is not any worse than the cost of putting a five-membered ring into the sheet.

So with a combination of five- and six- and seven-membered rings, you can take this one-atom-thick membrane, and you can wrap it over any structure you can imagine. It seems to me to be a miracle that there's *any* atom in the periodic table that can do this. [It's even more scary that there is only one.] But there is only one—just carbon.

Once Dr. Smalley's imagination gets rolling, he can't help but think of ways in which these special carbon structures might be used—from a cure for deadly diseases to a new future for electric power generation.

For example, the HIV [human immunodeficiency virus] that is currently thought to cause AIDS [acquired immune deficiency syndrome] is a little tiny object that is only about 100 nanometers in size. When it gets into your bloodstream, it goes throughout your body and enters individual cells. There, the coat on the outside of this virus particle comes off and the insides get out into your cells . . . [enabling the virus to reproduce].

In order to attack the HIV virus, you need something that gets into the body along with the virus and can intercept some critical stage of the life cycle of that virus.

The trick is to disrupt the virus without interfering with the body's normal functions. Some researchers believe that it may be possible to create a drug that will prevent HIV from reproducing by attaching key molecules to buckyballs. In such a scenario, the buckyball would act like a tiny transport module.

That's one idea. Another has to do with superconductors. There's a tremendous problem in our civilization of making electrical power. . . . One of the problems is transmitting it from one place to another on wires. Wires have resistance, and we lose power. We would love to have power cables that have no resistance whatsoever. There are such things in the world. They're called superconductors, . . . but we don't know how to make these superconductors work at room temperature.

It's been found that buckyballs mixed with other materials produce a superconductor that [works at] quite a high temperature [but still well below room temperature]. There's a lot of research going on right now to find a way of explaining why they superconduct and then to suggest ways of changing the ball to increase the temperature of that superconductivity.

We don't know yet whether you can make a practical room-temperature superconductor out of buckyballs—my guess is that you can, but there are a whole bunch of other structures that you can build with this motif. One of our favorites is [a long tube or] fiber. It turns out that if you pulled along [the length of] this tube to find out how much [force can be applied] before it breaks—the tensile strength—it would end up being . . . the strongest fiber ever made. We expect it would be a hundred times stronger than steel. . . . It would be a great thing to build with [or to put into composite materials]. . . .

There's a good chance that a cable made of buckytubes that are *doped* with a metal could have an electrical resistance that's a hundred to a thousand times smaller than the best conductor we know of right now: gold or copper. [Because doped buckytubes are strong, lightweight, and excellent conductors, they could easily replace current power grids.]

Probably none of the things I just told you will work out [exactly as I have described them], but because carbon is such a special element and because the structure [of a buckytube] is so special, . . . I'd be amazed if [many] years go by before bucky-related things become one of the major building blocks of high technology. . . .

Smalley's enthusiasm is contagious and is, no doubt, a major reason for his success in research. He traces some of that to the one scientist he knew when growing up, yet, oddly, not to that scientist's work. When you hear him talk first about that scientist and then about his own development as a person, you realize the importance of having a person or persons after whom you can model yourself.

My aunt, Sara Jane Rhoades, my mother's sister, was a professor of chemistry at the University of Wyoming. I had loved her for years. I thought she was the most impressive human being I ever met. But I didn't really quite know much about what she did. . . . She was a very warm, personable person, much more sociable than I thought I would ever be . . . interested in ideas, and had a very strong, independent career.

One of the things that I have discovered in my learning about people is that almost every person has some great virtues.

Smalley knows the importance of having someone to admire. He describes his aunt Sara Jane Rhoades, a professor of chemistry at the University of Wyoming, as "the most impressive human being I ever met, . . . warm, personal, . . . much more sociable than I thought I would ever be, . . . interested in ideas. [She] had a very strong, independent career."

Perhaps that is why Dr. Smalley enjoys working with students, and why so many young people find him a worthy model for themselves. When advising young people, he often recalls a mediocre high school student from Kansas City, Missouri, named Richard Smalley. That young man never earned an "A" grade until he took chemistry in eleventh grade and didn't decide to go to college until after he had graduated from high school and was working in a job that didn't seem quite right.

Basically, all I did was clean bottles and clean up spills and make myself famous for making spills—and rather obnoxious ones. I started to get into [science], initially driven by the fact that I was looking for something I could do well enough that I could make a job out of it.

But from the more romantic side, I think we were all, in those days, very intrigued by the notion that this is really where the action was. We all wanted to be astronauts, do anything we could possibly do to get our bodies into space! I never actually figured out how to do that. . . .

Before that, I wanted to be an architect. Before *that*, I wanted to be an opera singer. Luckily I found [a job] that I could actually do.

With experiences like those in Dr. Smalley's past, it is little wonder that he relates well to the normal uncertainties of young people like you. If you see yourself as a scientist, yet you wonder whether you are smart enough, talented enough, or dedicated enough to be successful, remember Dr. Smalley, and remember this piece of advice:

When you're still in high school, you're still very much in the process of becoming. Even when I was in my twenties—even in my thirties—I had not really begun to understand what it is like to be Rick Smalley. So when you're fifteen or so, give yourself a break. You don't have to solve all these problems today.

Chapter Four

Mapping What Makes Us Human: The Human Genome Project

DNA's a molecular code
In a long double-helical mode
They untwist its wrap,
Turn it into a map
Of our genome, that is, not a road.

Scientists often discuss "big science" and "little science." By big science, they mean massive projects, such as the space program, which involves large numbers of people and many millions, or even billions, of dollars. Little science involves only a few people. Frank Asaro, Helen Michel, and Richard Smalley are all working on projects that are considered little science.

In most ways, whether scientists work on big or little projects, their jobs and lives are quite similar, because big questions are usually answered one small step at a time. Still, this book would not be complete without looking at one of the biggest scientific quests ever: the Human Genome Project, an international effort that began in 1990 and is scheduled to last 15 years. In the United States, which is playing a leading role in the project, the $3-billion effort is headquartered at the National Center for Human Genome Research (NCHGR) on the campus of the National Institutes of Health (NIH) in Bethesda, Maryland (just north of Washington, D.C.). Scientists in hospitals and universities across the country are also involved.

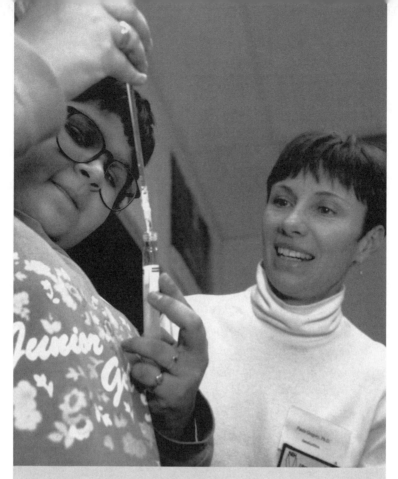

Paula Gregory loves science and loves to teach. Here she is spooling DNA with a group of girl scouts.

The scientists you will meet in this chapter have one common characteristic that distinguishes them from all the other scientists in this book. When talking about their work, they are far less likely than the others to bring personal experiences or beliefs into the discussion. As a result, this chapter has a different "flavor" from all the others; it discusses the science more heavily and tells less about the individual scientists' lives and personalities.

Why the difference? We can only speculate. Perhaps the large scale of the Human Genome Project dwarfs the individual scientists' pieces of it, so they think less about themselves when they think of the work. Perhaps working with human research subjects focuses their thoughts on the lives of those people rather than on their own lives. Perhaps—and this is the most speculative suggestion—people who go into health-related research have different personality traits from other scientists, and these interviews reflect that. Most likely it was simple chance that of all the scientists interviewed for this book, the ones at NCHGR were the least likely to talk about themselves.

Rather than speculating, however, let's leave that as an open question for further research. Instead, let's listen to what these NCHGR scientists had to say about the Human Genome Project as a whole, and where they fit into the grand scheme.

"The project was set up to try to identify and to *map* all the genes that make up a human being," explains Dr. Paula E. Gregory, Chief of Genetics Education for NCHGR. "That's somewhere around 100,000 genes."

What does Dr. Gregory mean when she speaks of mapping genes? That requires a bit of explanation.

As you probably know, all living organisms are made up of cells. In the center of each cell is a region called the *nucleus*, which acts as the control center for the cell's work. Within the nucleus are several sausage-like structures known as *chromosomes*. The number of chromosomes in the nucleus varies from one type of organism to another. Normal humans have twenty-three pairs of chromosomes, or forty-six chromosomes altogether. One member of each chromosome pair is *inherited* from the person's mother and the other member of the pair comes from the person's father.

Each chromosome carries units called *genes*. Genes influence the development and functioning of every body part and system. Some characteristics, such as a person's eye color, are determined by a single gene or pair of genes. Other characteristics, such as a person's tendency to grow tall or short or to develop certain talents and abilities, arise from the influence of many genes. Certain genes or combinations of genes may cause or *predispose* a person to inherited diseases.

By the middle of the twentieth century, scientists had learned a great deal about genes by studying patterns of inheritance in various organisms. They knew that certain chromosomes carry certain genes. They also knew that organisms grow and develop through a process called *mitosis*, or cell division. In this process, a "parent cell" divides to form two identical "daughter cells." Each new daughter cell contains chromosomes that are identical to those in the original parent cell.

Scientists also knew that chromosomes are made up of huge, complex molecules of *deoxyribonucleic acid*, or DNA. Still, they didn't know exactly how chromosomes carry their genes or how they reproduce themselves. This changed in 1953 when James Watson and Francis Crick determined the structure of DNA. They built a model showing that DNA molecules resemble long twisted ladders. Each "leg" of the ladder takes the form of a loosely coiled spring, called a *helix*. The

PAULA E. GREGORY

Current field of work: Genetics Education

Business title and mailing address: Chief of Genetics Education, National Center for Human Genome Research, National Institutes of Health, 49 Convent Drive, Bethesda, MD 20892

Date and place of birth: July 29, 1956, Edenton, NC

Education: B.S., University of Southern Mississippi, 1977; M. S., University of Southern Mississippi, 1979; Ph.D., Tulane University, 1990

Significant accomplishments:

- Made a key discovery regarding the disease process in neurofibromatosis (Elephant Man's Disease).
- Developed and leads the Education and Outreach program of the National Center for Human Genome Research.

Previously worked as: Researcher, teacher

Words of wisdom: Find what you're good at. Find what excites you. Pursue that, but be open to what we call "cross-training.". . . It's no longer OK to be just a physicist or just a molecular biologist. . . . You need to be more than one thing.

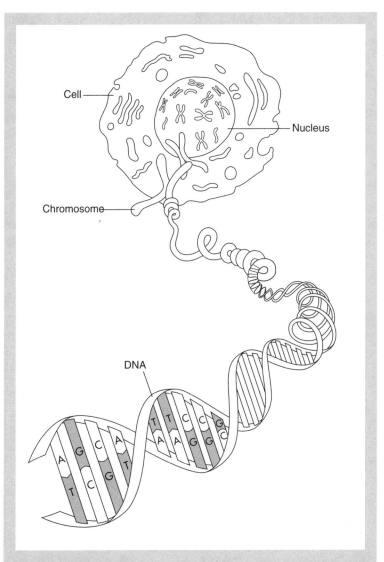

James Watson's and Francis Crick's 1953 model of the DNA molecule helped scientists understand the relationship between genes and chromosomes. Each rung of the double helix contains a matched pair of the nucleotide bases. Guanine (G) always pairs with cytosine (C) and thymine (T) always pairs with adenine (A). Each gene is characterized by a particular sequence of bases.

"rungs" of the ladder, which connect the two legs, are made of simple chemical units, called *nucleotides*. There are just four different nucleotides: adenine (A), thymine (T), cytosine (C), and guanine (G).

Each rung of the ladder consists of two nucleotides that are joined together. The nucleotides combine in only two ways, A with T and C with G. Thus, if you know the sequence of nucleotides attached to one leg of the ladder, you automatically know the sequence of nucleotides attached to the other leg of the ladder.

When a cell divides, the DNA of each chromosome splits like a zipper into two separate pieces. One half of the DNA ladder goes to each of the two new cells. The new cells contain all the materials necessary to rebuild the other half of the double helix.

Watson and Crick recognized that the sequence of nucleotides on a strand of DNA determines a person's genetic traits. The sequence of nucleotides varies from one person to another, but the most important parts of it are the same in all humans.

Since the Watson-Crick breakthrough, enormous scientific effort has gone into trying to identify the location and DNA sequence of certain genes, especially the ones responsible for diseases. In a way, this effort has been like creating an atlas, or collection of road maps, of the *human genome*.

To find the location of a gene, scientists first determine on which chromosome it resides. This step is like turning to a particular page in an atlas. Then they try to pin down its exact location by finding a nearby *marker*. (Researchers have studied each chromosome and identified particular points, or markers, on each one. These markers are spaced more or less evenly along each chromosome.) This step is like finding its general location on the map.

In the language of the Human Genome Project, the road map of markers on chromosomes is known as a *genetic map*. If you need to locate a gene more precisely, you can use a *physical map*, which specifies the gene's position by counting the number of nucleotide base pairs between it and a particular

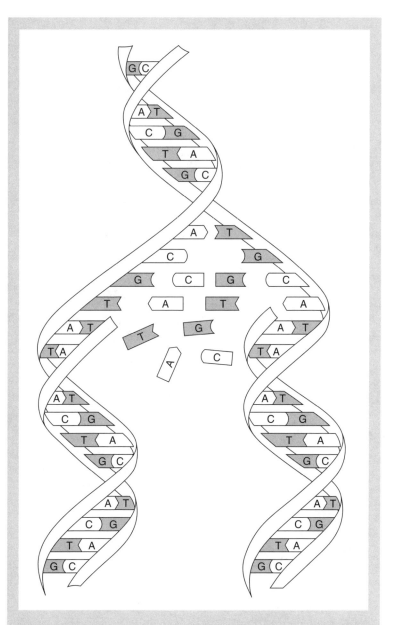

Cells reproduce by splitting into two identical new cells. When this happens, DNA must split too. The double helix "unzips" itself and each nucleotide base pairs up with a new partner. Those new partner bases have been manufactured within the organism from its food.

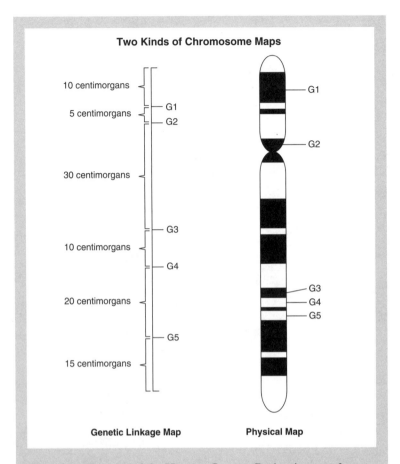

Two Kinds of Chromosome Maps

10 centimorgans

5 centimorgans — G1 / G2

30 centimorgans

G3

10 centimorgans

G4

20 centimorgans

G5

15 centimorgans

Genetic Linkage Map

G1

G2

G3
G4
G5

Physical Map

The major objective of the Human Genome Project is to produce maps that show the location of the genes on each chromosome. A genetic linkage map shows researchers how far a particular gene is from well-known markers. A physical map locates genes more precisely by specifying the number of base pairs between it and a particular marker.

marker. This process is like finding a dot that locates a town on a map. If you need to find your way around that town, then you go to a list of all of the town's streets, or, in some cases, all of its homes and buildings. Scientists determine the nucleotide sequence of a gene in a similar way.

When Dr. Gregory speaks of mapping the complete human genome, she is envisioning an atlas with a set of pages that contains the genetic map for each chromosome, another set of pages with physical maps showing the precise location of all 100,000 genes on those chromosomes, and a third set of pages listing the DNA sequence of each gene. The average gene has about 2,000 base pairs.

If you've been doing your arithmetic, you may be wondering about something. The average gene has 2,000 base pairs, and there are 100,000 genes. Therefore the human genome must contain a total of 200 million base pairs. What about the rest of the 6 billion base pairs in the genome? Dr. Gregory explains:

> [In] the average gene, the coding part is usually about 2,000 bases. [This coding region] has the recipe [that the cell uses to manufacture *proteins,* which carry out cellular activities]. Then there's . . . non-coding parts. . . . [Nearly] 95 percent of the genome, it's estimated, is non-coding.

These non-coding regions, which interrupt the coding regions, are scattered here and there within genes. The Human Genome Project focuses mostly on the coding portions of genes. According to Dr. Gregory,

> Coding [portions of] genes vary only the slightest bit, probably somewhere around 1 percent, from one person to the next. All the stuff in between, which makes up 95 percent of the human genome, is the stuff that differs. I call it "treasures in the attic." It's inherited in your family. Whatever your parents used to put in their attic is probably similar to what you put in your attic. What you put in your attic and your brother puts in his attic may be similar, but not identical. [The non-coding parts] can be unique to individuals. That's what they're using for *forensics* [identifying individuals in court through their DNA].

The scientific work is fascinating, but fascination alone would not justify spending $3 billion and employing thousands of scientists for one-third of their professional lives. The reason for spending all that money and effort, explains Dr. Gregory, is that it promises to produce vastly improved lives and health for millions of people.

> The focus here on [the NIH] campus is actually identifying and studying human disease genes. It's complementary to what is being done [at the other research sites across the country] because they're making the maps that we use to identify the disease genes. We are [also] identifying lots of genes that get added to the map that have nothing to do with disease. If you're hunting for the disease gene, you find lots of other things in there. . . .
>
> We take this basic information—this map of the genome—and immediately here on campus begin to apply it to human health. What are the genes that cause certain diseases; how can we begin to study what they do, and how can we then alleviate that genetic disease?
>
> The most immediate outcome [from finding] a human disease gene is a diagnostic [test] for that gene. You can begin testing for affected individuals [before they show symptoms of the disease or even before birth].
>
> Also, when you figure out what causes [a disease], you can sometimes come up with a better drug.

Dr. Richard (Rick) A. Morgan and his team of researchers is involved in the effort to treat, and perhaps to find a cure for AIDS. They are also searching for a treatment for hemophilia, an inherited condition in which the body fails to manufacture a protein necessary for blood clotting. They hope to treat both conditions by creating human-made viruses that deliver useful genetic material into the DNA of infected or genetically defective cells. Their hope is that the treated cells will then reproduce in such a way as to cure the disease or eliminate its harmful effects. This process is called *gene therapy*.

Gene therapy is a controversial procedure. Some people are afraid that the science will be abused to *clone*—or produce genetically identical—people. Others fear that misguided "mad

Rick Morgan's love of chemistry in high school led him to bio-chemistry and then to a career in molecular biology.

scientists" will alter human reproductive cells in an attempt to produce a "Master Race" or an inferior class of slaves.

Such fears are largely founded in misunderstanding of the science and are often reinforced by popular films and books. Still, scientists and management at NCHGR have not simply dismissed them. Rather they have created Dr. Gregory's office to educate the public about the possibilities and—more importantly—the limits of the science.

The Human Genome Project includes a scientific ethics component. The people working in this area seek ways to safeguard the research from abuse. Especially important is ensuring the privacy of individual medical and genetic information. If such information falls into the wrong hands, lives can be dis-

RICHARD A. MORGAN

Current field of work: Gene Therapy for AIDS

Business title and mailing address: Chief, Gene Transfer Technology Section, Clinical Gene Therapy Branch, National Center for Human Genome Research, National Institutes of Health, 10 Center Drive, Building 10, Room 10C103, Bethesda, MD 20892

Date and place of birth: March 20, 1959, Marblehead, MA

Education: B.A., Biochemistry, Brandeis University, 1981, Ph.D., Genetics, The Johns Hopkins University, 1987

Significant accomplishments:

- W. R. Grace Fellowship as outstanding graduate student in the Department of Biology, The Johns Hopkins University, 1984 and 1985.
- National Hemophilia Foundation Research Service Award, 1992.
- Development of gene transfer vectors (viruslike entities that transfer new genetic information into the DNA of living cells).

Words of wisdom: Keep an open mind and don't focus too soon on one thing. . . . Don't decide in the eleventh grade that you want to be a chemical engineer. I think that's the worst thing you can do. If you like science, you'll find [an area that's right]—or it will find you.

rupted or ruined. That sort of abuse is far more likely than the fictitious images of *The Boys from Brazil* (a novel and movie in which escaped Nazi scientists create their vision of a master race—hundreds of boys cloned from the genes of Adolf Hitler.)

> **Morgan:** There are a lot of misconceptions about gene therapy. It isn't about cloning organisms. It's not about creating a perfect organism. . . . It's really about treating disease. It's about trying . . . [to understand] how the molecules of your cells work—to use that knowledge to try to engineer, if you will, the cells from a person who has a disease . . . to fight that disease.
>
> **Gregory:** There's not anyone we've met—other than maybe

my babysitter—that I want to clone. We're really not cloning people. We're not even cloning parts of people. We are cloning specific segments of DNA. . . .

[Gene therapy is] just another kind of medical technology. . . . This is not anything different from doing balloon angioplasty [a common procedure used to clear a blocked artery] or bypass surgery; it's just a new kind of medical treatment. For some diseases, it may be really the most effective [form of treatment].

One such disease is hemophilia.

Morgan: [Hemophilia is the result of] a defect in one single protein that comes from one single gene. . . . The way hemophiliacs treat themselves now is [by injecting] clotting factors, which they get from their pharmacies, into their veins. . . .

[The missing protein in hemophilia] is a huge molecule. . . . You couldn't synthesize it [chemically, but] you can make it by *recombinant DNA,* and that's what they're doing now. [Scientists] are actually producing the protein [using bacteria that has had the human clotting factor gene inserted into its DNA].

If scientists working at pharmaceutical companies can insert the human clotting factor gene into bacteria, perhaps it would be possible to insert it into the cells of a hemophiliac's liver. If the gene would function in the liver and reproduce when the liver cells divide, the person's hemophilia would be cured. Unfortunately, inserting the human clotting factor gene into a person is not as simple as inserting it into a bacterium.

That's where the synthetic viruses developed by Dr. Morgan's group come in.

[We rely] on what nature has given us to transfer genes most effectively—viruses. Using recombinant DNA and microbiology tricks, we go into [a] mouse virus and throw out the disease genes. . . . [In their place, we] put in one of

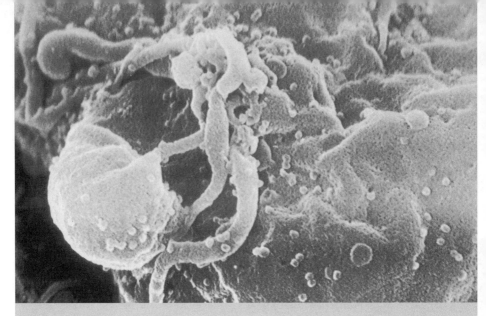

This electron micrograph shows a cancer-causing virus (left) budding from a T-lymphocyte. The human immunodeficiency virus (HIV), which causes AIDS, reproduces and spreads in much the same way.

these human clotting factor genes. So now we have a synthetic virus, which is no longer infectious (disease-causing) but is just used to deliver genes. We're now trying to figure out the most effective ways to deliver these synthetic viruses to the liver cells.

Dr. Morgan adds that the same synthetic viruses, with different genes spliced, or inserted, into them, may also be useful in the treatment of AIDS. HIV, the virus that causes AIDS, infects and eventually destroys a particular kind of infection-fighting white blood cell known as the *T-lymphocyte.* The T-cells are a major part of keeping your immune system working. That's why the immune system is slowly destroyed over the course of HIV infection.

Before an infected T-lymphocyte dies, it serves as a place where the HIV virus can reproduce. Dr. Morgan and his group hope to create a *synthetic* virus that will infect and alter a person's blood-producing cells in such a way that the new T-cells will no longer enable HIV to reproduce.

All of your blood cells come from one simple cell, which as it divides, or differentiates, turns from one primitive cell type into a more complex cell type. That cell, called a *stem cell*, is in your bone marrow. We know almost certainly that the HIV virus does not get into that stem cell.

[Our approach involves delivering] our synthetic virus into the stem cell. [The synthetic virus will] make a protein that will [prevent HIV from reproducing without affecting] the biology of the cell—how it divides, how one cell turns into a red blood cell, how [another] turns into a lymphocyte. So we're trying to use these synthetic viruses to block the replication of HIV.

Dr. Morgan explains that developing and testing that synthetic virus is a multi-step process involving both laboratory work and human testing.

We know in the laboratory that we can block HIV from replicating in mature T-cells. If we can show we can also do that in a patient, then we can go back and [try to] protect the stem cell so that all the T-cells . . . will potentially be resistant to HIV infection.

Another NCHGR group is interested in T-cells and the immune system, but for a different reason. Its leader is Dr. R. Michael Blaese, a pediatrician whose research always has a direct connection to the patients under his care. His patients are children with severe immune deficiencies.

Blaese: I am a physician, and I have been doing clinical research for my entire career. . . . For the last 30 years, I have been taking care of children who are born into this world without the ability to defend themselves against this sea of microorganisms that we all live in.

There are about thirty different inherited or genetic diseases that have major problems with immunity. Perhaps the most famous child is David, "the Bubble Boy," who was born with a disease called severe combined immune deficiency. David's disease is one of the kinds of things that I take care of.

Unlike Dr. Morgan, who became interested in gene therapy research because it was an interesting area of science, Dr. Blaese chose it because it was a promising way to help his patients.

I got involved in gene therapy, [because it] was an area of science that was developing to the point that there might be a chance [to help patients]. We had run into a blind alley for treating many of [them].

Genes are the information molecules of life, and we knew that genetic disease was caused by a misspelling of the code; typos in the sequence of DNA would somehow lead to disease. I decided to figure out if we could use a gene from a normal person to somehow treat patients who had been born with a misspelled gene.

That problem has an enormous number of associated problems: How are we going to go about getting the gene into the cells? Is it going to be safe? How is it going to be

Michael Blaese considers himself a pediatrician first and a researcher second. After 30 years in medicine and research, he continues to draw inspiration from his patients and their families.

regulated? Can you use anybody's gene or do you have to get a parent's gene? . . .

As we got into the whole science of transferring genes from one organism to another, it became more and more apparent that we might be able to use *gene transfer* not only to treat genetic disease, but we could actually use it to treat almost any disease. Acquired disorders that we don't think of as being genetic—things such as cancer or diabetes or even AIDS . . . might be attacked by using gene therapy.

It became more and more exciting as we began to think about the potential of this kind of treatment, if only we could figure out a way of getting it to work. So we focused on one very, very rare immune problem that—at least to our thinking about a decade ago—had the best combination of features to [show] that this idea of gene therapy might work.

In 1990, a 4-year-old girl with severe combined immune deficiency became the first person to undergo an authorized human gene therapy procedure. The patient had a condition similar to David's, except that it was caused by a defect in a different enzyme. This time the missing enzyme was adenosine deaminase (ADA).

It happened that just at the time when we thought this would be a good disease [to study], somebody cloned the gene [for the ADA enzyme] and made [it] available to us. . . . We could go ahead and try to develop ways [of adding healthy genes into the patient cells].

After receiving a dozen treatments, one-half of the girl's immune system cells contained healthy copies of the gene that directs the production of the ADA enzyme. Although more time is needed to determine how successful ADA gene therapy is, the preliminary results look promising.

Drs. Gregory, Morgan, and Blaese are only three of thousands of scientists working for or with NCHGR. Some peo-

R. MICHAEL BLAESE

Current field of work: Gene Therapy

Business title and mailing address: Chief, Clinical Gene Therapy Branch, National Center for Human Genome Research, National Institutes of Health, Building 10, Room 10C103, Bethesda, MD 20892-1852

Date and place of birth: February 16, 1939, Minneapolis, MN

Education: B. S., Gustavus Adolphus College, 1961, M.D., University of Minnesota, 1964

Significant accomplishments:

- Headed research team that performed the first human gene therapy procedure on a 4-year-old child with ADA deficiency (David's—Bubble Boy—Disease).
- Developed gene therapy for brain tumors.
- Discovered that "suppressor T-cells" can contribute to human disease.

Previously worked as: Immunologist, pediatrician

Words of wisdom: Think back on all of the other people that have ever lived on the face of the earth: how few have had the luxury of choosing what they could do with their career. That's [an opportunity] we have now. . . . [So choose] something you really love for your career. It is a privilege that you shouldn't squander.

ple might say that the result of the project will be a map of what makes us human; but most scientists on the project know that your DNA merely makes you a particular person. There's more to being human than that.

Part of being human is being ethical in your work and in your actions. Dr. Gregory takes great pride in NCHGR's commitment to ethical concerns.

We are unique in that we have an ethical, legal, and social implications program that gives grants and provides money for research into the ethics of the science. This is the first time there's been an ethics part of a [major government] science project from the very beginning.

The ethical implications are vast, and some of them will have no resolution. What we're really worried about are the legal and policy issues, because there are very few laws that govern the use of genetic information, or the misuse of genetic information, or the privacy of genetic information.

So we've commissioned task forces and studies to actually look at this. Five percent of our total budget goes into this ethics program. [Author's note: Do your arithmetic here. Five percent of $3 billion = $150 million over 15 years, a considerable sum, to say the least!]

Another part of being human is caring about the people in your life and those who may follow in your footsteps. When asked to speak directly to the young scientists, Drs. Gregory, Morgan, and Blaese each spoke in their own way about the importance of discovering your own gifts and making choices that enable you to use those gifts well.

Paula Gregory, who is a gifted communicator as well as a solid scientific researcher, pointed out the importance of learning to do more than one thing well.

Find what you're good at. Find what excites you. Pursue that, but be open to what we call "cross-training.". . . It's no longer OK to be just a physicist or just a molecular biologist. You need to be a molecular biologist who knows a lot about databases or who knows all about computers. You need to be more than one thing.

Rick Morgan, who continues to discover new areas that fascinate him, warns against making long-term choices too early in life.

Keep an open mind and don't focus too soon on one thing. For example, I was very good in chemistry in high school and thought I was going to pursue that, but when I found out what biochemistry was all about, I found that much more interesting. Biochemistry led to molecular biology.

So I think you have to keep an open mind. You may have an interest in biology, but in the college environment, find out more about the other sciences. . . . Don't decide in the eleventh grade that you want to be a chemical engineer. I think that's the worst thing you can do. If you like science, you'll find [an area that's right]—or it will find you.

Michael Blaese, whose life-saving work has given many desperately ill children the opportunity to live a normal life, speaks of making the most of the opportunities you have been given.

Think back on all of the other people that have ever lived on the face of the earth: how few have had the luxury of choosing what they could do with their career. That's [an opportunity] we have now. We don't have to go out into the field and hunt and plow every day. [So choose] something you really love for your career. It is a privilege that you shouldn't squander.

A visit with the scientists at NCHGR can teach you a great deal about the scientific basis of human life. These scientists can help you see the value in creating a detailed map, 200 million letters long, of the human genome. Their unscientific thoughts also have value. Those thoughts speak not about life, but rather about living: Be human. Discover your gifts. Choose well.

Chapter Five

Patricia Wattenmaker: Piecing Together the History of Civilization

A city was there long ago.
Old animal bones tell her so.
Though some think she's quirky
For digging in Turkey,
She insists that there's much more to know.

University of Virginia Anthropologist Patricia Wattenmaker could not be more different from the scientists at the National Center for Human Genome Research discussed in Chapter 4—or more the same. NCHGR scientists are part of a team of thousands of people working on a multibillion-dollar effort; Dr. Wattenmaker works on projects about one ten-thousandth that size. NCHGR scientists work in ultraclean, climate-controlled laboratories with the most sophisticated modern equipment; Dr. Wattenmaker does much of her work in the hot sun or the rain, and digs her scientific samples out of the soil of southeastern Turkey. NCHGR scientists work with living people and cells; Dr. Wattenmaker works with objects—many in bits and pieces—found in the cities, villages, and homes of people who have been dead for thousands of years.

Yet both NCHGR scientists and Dr. Wattenmaker seek answers to important questions about what makes us human. At NCHGR, they seek to understand the biological basis of our species by studying the molecular code of human DNA. In Dr. Wattenmaker's work, she seeks to understand the development of human civilization and culture by studying the archaeological remains of the homes of everyday people. Both tasks require painstaking work to assemble thousands of pieces until a broader picture becomes apparent. Both require persistence, dedication, highly developed skills, and a mind prepared to recognize unexpected opportunities.

Anthropologist and archaeologist Patricia Wattenmaker, Assistant Professor in the University of Virginia's Anthropology Department, reads the history and economic development of ancient civilizations in animal bones and other artifacts.

Unexpected events and a prepared mind played particularly important roles at the beginning of Dr. Wattenmaker's career and in a major discovery several years later.

I view it as almost an accident that I'm an archaeologist rather than a cultural anthropologist studying living groups. . . . I was always fascinated with archaeology, and I chose a college that had an archaeology program, but I really didn't think it was something you could do for a living; but once I got involved in it, I really got hooked. . . .

A real pivotal point for me was as an undergraduate [college student]. I was majoring in anthropology, and I did volunteer work at the University of Michigan in the Museum of Anthropology, working with a graduate student on animal bones.

This happened just because I had wandered into the museum and asked the director if there was some volunteer work I could do. He said talk to this graduate student and see if she needs some help—Dr. [Melinda] Zeder, who's now at the Smithsonian. I started working with her on some animal bones that she had brought back from Iran for her dissertation work.

That was my first real experience with hands-on research. It was very rewarding, because we were getting answers, but [it was] pivotal because I also picked up a skill in analyzing animal remains.

Animal bones found in human settlements can indicate, among other things, what kind of animals the people were raising, how they used them for food, and how they butchered them. As you will read later on, the bones can provide clues to the culture and economy, not just the people's food production and eating habits.

Archaeologists often bring the bones found in the field back to their home laboratory for careful scientific analysis that would not be possible at the site of their excavation, or "dig." The skills Dr. Wattenmaker developed in her volunteer work in the museum soon—and unexpectedly—led to her first experience in the field.

> There was another student, an undergraduate at the University of Michigan, who was planning on going on a project in Morocco studying animal bones. For personal reasons, [she] had to change her plans. . . . [She and] Mindy Zeder thought that maybe I could go instead of her.
>
> I had never been in the field. I'd never done any of this on my own. I was just really assisting Mindy, and they asked me, "Do you want to go to Morocco?" And, being adventurous—I wasn't sure where Morocco exactly was—I said, "Sure!" . . .
>
> Then I was off during my senior year at college to undertake the bone analysis on a site in Morocco. That was terrifying, quite honestly, because I had never done that kind of thing on my own. I got there, and I wasn't sure what to do. The work was slow going, but in the end I got a letter of commendation out of it; and I had gotten so involved in my work at that point that it would have been difficult for me not to go on in archaeology.

Dr. Wattenmaker had the preparedness of mind to recognize an opportunity and the courage to accept it, even though she recognized that she had a lot to learn. (In Chapter 6, Dr. Roberta Nichols tells about a woman engineer who similarly had the courage to accept an opportunity even though it meant learning and occasionally embarrassing herself in full view of a mostly male group of technicians.) That preparedness and courage would serve Dr. Wattenmaker well again years later, when she decided to take on the excavation of a major site in southeastern Turkey called Kazane Höyük, a site she is still studying today.

To understand what she has found there and why it has been so important to her, you must begin with her particular approach to research. Once you understand how she views her work, you will be able to appreciate how a small research project led her first to her doctoral dissertation, and then to Kazane.

Each scientist has a different way of answering questions. I've tried to take a very synthetic approach from the point of view of data [putting together different pieces of evidence].

Archaeology tends to be a very specialized field. Some people might be specialists in pottery, for example; other people might be specialists in animal bones; other people might direct excavations but not conduct any *artifact* analysis.

I've tried to develop a number of different skills so that I can piece together all the different lines of evidence and get a more holistic picture of the societies that I have studied. I've found that oft-times when I'm trying to answer a question, one line of evidence—such as pottery or animal bones—is completely inadequate. Whereas, when I have many lines of evidence—architecture, spatial layout of the settlement, stone tools, objects, ornaments—I start to see a much broader picture.

[Author's note: Dr. Wattenmaker's comments here echo those of Dr. Paula Gregory of NCHGR, who points out the importance of being good at more than one thing.]

The very first research project that I started in southeastern Turkey was a small town located very close to the site I'm working on now. I started out as the animal bone specialist. This was a small town. The area was believed to be a very peripheral area [on the outer edge of Sumerian civilization]. Some people called it "the exit ramp of the Middle East." It was not known for having large settlements.

In my study of the animal bones, I picked up a lot of specialization in the food production system. [Farmers specialized in raising one or a few kinds of animals and therefore had a surplus to trade with others.] That [was unexpected. It] did not fit the model of a small-town site in a peripheral area. Even in the heartlands of cities, like some [other archaeologists had found] in Iraq, the model was that smaller village sites with non-elite houses tended to have household autonomy. [That is, the common people tended to raise all of their own food, rather than specializing in one product and trading surpluses for other products.]

Individual farms were raising their own food, raising their own animals, farming. [The people] were not really involved in an urban economy that you get with early civilization—[an economy] where you've got traders, you've got craft specialists, a lot of exchange. That [kind of economy] was seen as an exclusively elite phenomenon. The elite people were getting all the goods produced by these craft specialists. Whereas the non-elite households were making all their own crafts and all their own food.

That was the model I was working from, but [the bones told a different story]. I noticed that there was a lot of [evidence of] specialization in food production in the animal bones. That led me to my dissertation topic, which was: What happens to these non-elite households when you get a state society [with a strong central government]? Is it true that they are not really involved in this state system—that they continue to produce their food and their crafts unaffected by this really fundamental shift in the way society was organized? Or was this an indicator that I was picking up a hint of something more major, that the families were really drawn into a specialized urban economy?

For my dissertation, I moved from the animal bones to actually excavating some non-elite houses and studying not just the animal bones, but also the pottery and the chipped stone, the spatial layout of the houses and any objects that I found in the houses, like jewelry, figurines. [As I went, I kept] asking . . . how these houses changed with state society.

What I found was very different from expectations about these non-elite houses. I found that the non-elite families did indeed become an integral part of the urban economy, not only producing specialized goods, but also consuming a lot of specialized goods, [although they still used a lot of goods they made themselves].

When I looked at the goods that were obtained from specialists versus the goods that the households were producing, I found that the highly visible kinds of goods that you would use in social situations where you would be sending messages to other people about your status, like vessels to serve guests or clothes that you would wear outside the home—those kinds of goods would be produced by specialists. Whereas the kinds of goods that would only be seen in the household by the family, like stone tools, were still produced by households.

So Dr. Wattenmaker had discovered, much to everyone's surprise, that today's consumer society had roots that went back much further in history than anyone had suspected. Even more surprising was that she had found this evidence in an area far from any known major city. That piece of the puzzle didn't seem to fit. She began to think that something was missing. Then, unexpectedly, she stumbled across a major find.

The most exciting moment in my career was finding the site I'm now working on. It was exciting for a number of different reasons. One was these households and the degree of specialization that I was finding. It made me think that we were missing a big part of the picture.

As I said, this area was viewed as a periphery; but even at the small site that I was working on, there was so much economic specialization in the non-elite households. I began to think that there was a large city somewhere that we were just not finding—that we were missing.

I hypothesized that maybe the site was to the southeast near the modern city of Sanhurfa [Urfa], but I really had no way of knowing that at the time. It was just that if you drive in that area, you can see that there are a lot of large sites. . . . We didn't know that any of these were early [sites]. It was just a suspicion that I had, but I never dreamed that I would ever find such a large site, if it had originally existed, partly because most of the early sites were buried under later [settlements, so] it would be very hard to even see. Early pottery, early architectural evidence is very deeply buried, sometimes under 12 meters [40 ft.] of debris, [because later civilizations would often build right on top of the ruins of earlier ones].

So I suspected it, but didn't ever really think that we'd

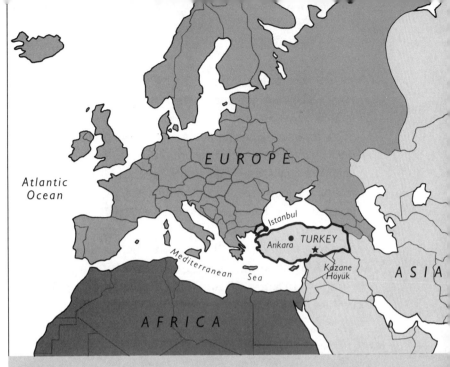

Wattenmaker stumbled across a major find at Kazane Höyük in southeastern Turkey. The site that had been overlooked despite the fact that it was visible from the rooms of a hotel she had been staying in for years.

find the answer. [Then,] when I was looking for a [new] site to excavate, I found what I believe is this center that I [had suspected] but thought I would never find—and it was completely by accident!

One of the real surprises to me was that this site was just about 3 kilometers [2 mi.] from the modern city of Urfa. You could actually see it from the roof of the hotel that we'd been staying in for 10 years. I myself had driven by it maybe ten or twenty times; but for a number of reasons, no one had ever realized how early the site was or how large it was.

From the angle we took driving up to the site, we [could not see its full size]. That's when I realized it was such a huge site, because the city wall was so flat [and long]. When we got out of the car and looked over the ground, it was littered with very early pottery.

I think what people had done in the past was driven right up to the high mound [of the city wall] and not looked on the ground around it. If you look [only] at the high mound, you don't see as much early pottery. It's buried and you don't know how rich the site is.

Looking back on the time before she discovered Kazane Höyük, Dr. Wattenmaker gives more details about why the site is so important and why she decided to tackle a project far larger than any she had ever planned to take on.

I had the notion that there was a big site there for several different reasons. First of all, I always felt that we were not excavating in the right areas. In the 1980s, there were a number of foreign projects along the Euphrates [River] in southeast Turkey, including two American projects. The sites were chosen—or the location to work was chosen—not necessarily because it was the richest area, but because that's where they were building the dams. So we were working right along the river where the sites would be flooded.

[Second,] I always wondered if we were not getting a biased sample. The sites along the river might be special-function sites, perhaps where they would trade or [have] a river crossing. The heartlands of settlement might be elsewhere. I knew that the area we were working in was relatively unexplored, and that the small area that was explored was not representative of the entire area. Thus, it could potentially be a highly biased sample.

A third indicator was the results that we found at those small sites. Even the poorest people at the settlement were really involved in a highly specialized economy. Now people tend not to get involved in a highly specialized economy, especially when it comes to food, unless they feel confident that the supply networks are in place, that trade systems are in place, transportation systems [are in place], and that takes a government state society.

I imagined that for such a specialized economy, there must be a regional center somewhere that was overseeing the system . . . .

Another indicator was that I was finding a lot of evidence for what we call a tributary economy, where households seemed to be paying taxes. They were producing surpluses that they were not consuming.

That wasn't really easy to pick out. I picked it up with the animal bones. We knew from texts elsewhere in Mesopotamia that people did pay their taxes in animals, one of the reasons being that animals can walk by themselves.

When I looked at the ages of the animals, [I discovered essentially none of] what we call the prime age category, where the animal reaches its maximum size. [At that point,] it's no longer worth the herder's effort to care for the animal, so they generally slaughter the animal at that age—about 2½ years.

I was finding [bones of] very young animals that perhaps died in infancy . . . and then older animals that were used for breeding. The fact that the prime-age animals were gone indicated to me that they were being sent somewhere, possibly as tributes [taxes]. That raised the question, "Where is the tribute going?"

Same thing with agriculture. It seemed like settlement [population density] was really pretty low. There shouldn't have been a strain on the land, and yet we were finding evidence [that there was].

Here's where teamwork comes in. I was doing the animal bones. There was an *ethnobotanist* working on the seed remains and a *geomorphologist* working on the environment surrounding the site. The geomorphologist was finding evidence for erosion, which indicates overuse of the land and deforestation. Also, he was finding evidence for intensive cultivation.

The ethnobotanist was also picking up the deforestation, and I was also picking up the deforestation in the sense that pigs were dropping out and goats were increasing. . . . [Author's note: pigs could forage the forest, but goats are grazing animals.]

So the question was: If they had plenty of land, as it seemed they did . . . why were they overusing the land? Presumably they were sending the surpluses elsewhere. All of these factors indicated to me that we were missing a major center.

That was my hunch [but it was still a surprise because] when I found Kazane, this lost center, I was not looking for a large site. It was going to be the first site that I would excavate on my own, and I was looking for something manageable, easy to find funding for.

But I also wanted to pursue the research questions that I had started with, so I was really looking for a small site from the same time period. I was intrigued with Kazane as we were driving by. The museum director told me that the site was going to be partially destroyed because they had constructed an irrigation canal through it. So when we stopped to look, it wasn't for me. I wasn't looking to excavate that site. I had always said that I would never tackle a big site.

But we were thinking, the site's going to be destroyed; perhaps we need to find someone who might want to take this site on. Then, once I got there and realized the significance of the site and that a large part of the site was going to be destroyed really soon—that it was really quite urgent—I changed my research aims and decided to take it on.

When Patricia Wattenmaker began her studies of archaeology, she loved the field but did not really expect to find a job in it. Had she given in to some people's advice to major in something where she could find a "real job," she would have missed out on all the accomplishments—and all the fun.

Some might call her lucky to have had the series of opportunities that have marked her career: working with Melinda Zeder; being able to accept the unexpected job opening for an animal bone specialist in Morocco; discovering the archaeological riches at Kazane Höyük. However, most good scientists would know that those were not simply "lucky breaks." Rather, they know that opportunities such as those come to everyone regularly, but unexpectedly. Those who have prepared themselves and believe in themselves seize their good fortune and build on it.

Dr. Wattenmaker puts it this way:

> Be open to your own interest and dreams. Believe in yourself; have confidence in yourself; and [be] true to yourself. If you want to do something, if you want to choose a field of science that is not necessarily practical or employable, you may find people trying to discourage you from that field. . . . But I believe that if you truly love what you do and really apply yourself, you can make an unconventional, difficult field work for you. You can find a place in that field.

Chapter Six

Roberta Nichols: Racing To Find the Engine of the Future

Some of us, Dr. Nichols has said.
From our childhood have wheels in our head.
She loves engines and fuels,
Laboratories and tools,
But she'd rather be racing instead.

All the other chapters of this book profile scientists who have spent most of their professional lives in university or government laboratories. This chapter is an exception, and its subject—Dr. Roberta Nichols, a scientist who discovered that she preferred to work in an industrial setting—is used to being exceptional.

Her career path—applied science and engineering in industry—is not unusual. More scientists earn their living that way than any other, although few are as successful as Roberta Nichols. Her achievements—both in engineering and in speedboat and auto racing—are exceptional by any standard; but what makes them even more remarkable is that she is a woman who came of age in the late 1940s and early 1950s.

Young women of that generation were rarely encouraged to pursue engineering careers, and most were actively discouraged from doing so. Furthermore, it was almost unheard-of for a girl to develop a hobby that would leave grease under her fingernails. None of that mattered to Roberta Nichols' father.

When asked to list her significant achievements, alternative fuel expert and former speedboat racing record-holder Roberta Nichols includes her two children and four grandchildren. Nichols' granddaughters Gina and Flora Lagatutta, shown here, must be the envy of their classmates for having a classic car-racing, snow-skiing grandma.

He was a great do-it-yourself person. He was a self-taught engineer; he did not have a college degree but functioned as an engineer. . . . He worked for 43 years at the Douglas Aircraft Company.

Because he was a great innovative kind of person—grew up on a farm, liked to fix things, worked on his own cars—I used to go to the junkyard and the welding shop, and we'd go fishing together, all kinds of things.

So I really grew up in a man's world. I didn't know I wasn't supposed to like all that stuff. That greatly influenced my life. He particularly had an innate love for cars, and had great cars. He had a '34 Plymouth that he drove back and forth to work, with a floor shift. That's the car I learned to drive in.

Although Dr. Nichols credits her father for getting her started, she acknowledges that her love of cars and engines, like his, is probably innate. It would have taken active discouragement to divert her from the path to becoming an automotive engineer. She quotes her husband, himself a classic-car enthusiast, to describe her compulsion to create and test high-performance engines.

> As my husband says, some of us are born with wheels in our head, and I think I'm one of those.

Today, young women born with wheels in their head have an easier time of it; but Dr. Nichols knows that they still have obstacles to overcome that their male counterparts do not. The advice she gives them, however, is useful to everyone.

> I have talked to a lot of young women through the Society of Women Engineers. One of the things that I [stress] is: Don't be afraid to try something. Don't be afraid that you're going to look silly if you don't know how to do it the first time.
>
> I had a woman working for me here at Ford. I didn't realize when I put her in charge of a project to develop an alternative fuel vehicle, which had a stick shift—a manual transmission—that she didn't know how to drive a car with a manual transmission. She learned—and she had to learn in view of the whole experimental garage. A few times, she went leaping out the door as the clutch got released a little bit too fast. But the point I'm making is she had the courage to try it, and pretty soon she did it very well.

Despite her love of cars, Dr. Nichols began her professional career as a mathematician in a missile engineering group at the Douglas Aircraft Company. After two job changes and several years, she was working as an engineer on Air Force space projects for the Aerospace Corporation.

Meanwhile, in her spare time, she was becoming known in the boat-racing world for her expertise in high-performance

Roberta Nichols racing her Drag Boat, the Witch, *circa 1966. Her speed of 131 miles per hour (210 km/hr.) over a quarter-mile (400 m) set a record for blown-fuel hydro class boats. The record was not topped for 3 years.*

engines. She knew everything about them: every part, every detail of their performance. She was especially knowledgeable about the chemical reactions that took place in the combustion chamber.

That knowledge and her physical skills in piloting speedboats enabled her to set a blown-fuel hydroplane speed record that stood for 3 years. She didn't realize it at the time, but that knowledge and skill was also about to launch her in a whole new career direction.

> At the Aerospace Corporation, we had seed money from our Air Force contracts, which allowed us to do research that was not directly connected with any of our Air Force space programs. To supplement [that] money, we decided to move into the civilian operations area.
>
> [The management] looked around the company for [people who] knew something about internal combustion

engines. I happened to be one of those, because I was very involved in boat racing and building high-performance engines.

We started a project [to develop] a high-octane gasoline without the use of lead. That was in the early '70s. The edict had been put out to take all the lead out of the gasoline. [Because of my experience with methanol [wood alcohol] in boat-racing engines, I knew that was a high-performance fuel.

So I did research on the use of methanol as a blending octane agent in gasoline. Some of that work came to the attention of the state of California, [which was very concerned about reducing air pollution from automobile exhaust]. Eventually, I did some consulting for them. I built a vehicle for the state of California that ran on methanol. It was a Ford Pinto.

I gave a paper on this project at a conference at which one of the directors of the Ford Scientific Research Laboratories was a session chair. I became known to him. . . . That led to Ford's interest in me and my knowledge. Eventually, I was invited to come to Ford to do engine research work for Ford of Brazil, where they were just moving into production of ethanol [grain alcohol]-fueled vehicles. That's how I moved from the space industry to Ford Motor Company.

During the 1970s and 1980s, U.S. and California government standards for air quality and fuel economy led Ford and the other major automobile manufacturers to develop alternative fuel engines. Roberta Nichols led that effort for Ford. She takes great pride in the fact that in the 1990s, the company moved her work from the research laboratory into production.

Because I had done that consulting work for California, my connection with the state of California and the Energy Commission remained in place, and Ford became the deliverer of alternative fuel vehicles for the state of California. In addition to the alcohol vehicles, we also did propane, natural gas. [We also did] paper studies on some of the

ROBERTA NICHOLS

Current field of work: Alternative Fuels/New Sources of Energy (retired from Ford Motor Company)

Business title and mailing address: Alternative Fuels Consultant, 8645 N. Territorial Rd., Plymouth, MI 48170-5043

Date and place of birth: November 29, 1931, Los Angeles, CA

Education: B.S., Physics, UCLA; M.S., Environmental Engineering, USC; Ph.D., Engineering, USC

Significant accomplishments:

- Author of more than fifty scientific and engineering articles.
- Holder of three patents for flexible fuel vehicles.
- Recipient of the National Achievement Award from Society of Women Engineers (their highest honor).
- First female elected as a Fellow of the Society of Automotive Engineers.
- Founding Member and Chairman of the Board for 8 years of the National Drag Boat Association.
- Holder of the water-speed record for drag boat racing for 3 years (blown-fuel hydroplane).
- President of Gull Wing Group International, Inc.
- Mother of two children, grandmother of four, still snow-skiing and vintage-car racing at age 64.

Previously worked as: Manager of Alternative Fuel Vehicle Development at Ford Motor Company, member of the Technical Staff at the Aerospace Corporation and at Space Technology Laboratory, Mathematician in Missiles Engineering at Douglas Aircraft Company

Words of wisdom: (1) Don't be afraid to try something. Don't be afraid that you're going to look silly if you don't know how to do it the first time. (2) If you can properly define the problem, you can find the solution. It's the definition of the problem that is often wrong, so people are searching for the wrong solution.

other alternatives, but did not actually build any hydrogen vehicles, for example.

The early work with the state of California really was

important to the success that eventually led to our being able to take these vehicles into production.

Looking back at more than two decades of work with Ford, Roberta Nichols has a number of interesting insights into the differences between work in industry and in "pure" science. She attributes much of her success to having developed "a firsthand knowledge of what the customer expects out of the vehicle."

Good research results do not mean that something is ready for the market. Without something that will be pleasing to the customer, nothing happens. In the auto industry, we have to be customer-driven, because it's an absolute fact that customers buy only what they want to buy.

In the case of the automobile, they expect a piece of equipment. They get in and turn the key, and it takes them from Point A to Point B every time. They expect it to be reliable, to do the same thing day after day. So when you make the transition to new sources of energy, you have to make [the changes in] the vehicle as transparent to the customer as possible. If it's too different from what they have been used to for years and years, or if it is inconvenient because it requires a lot more action on their part, they simply won't buy it. . . .

We learned this in the process of doing prototype fleets for the state of California, as well as a few other experimental programs throughout the world. By delivering alternative fuel vehicles to field service, we all learned what the user of the vehicle really expected and was willing to put up with.

For example, we had dedicated methanol vehicles [Author's note: That means vehicles that use only methanol as a fuel] that we sent to California, but the state of California had only eighteen methanol refueling stations. We had 500 methanol vehicles throughout the state. [The fueling stations were] strategically located; nevertheless, we gave a lot of drivers a lot of anxiety wondering if they were going to be able to do whatever they needed to do before they ran out of fuel or before they found the next methanol station.

As a consequence, we realized that it was very difficult to get dedicated vehicles and refueling stations in the field in sufficient numbers all at the same time. [So] we began to develop a flexible fuel vehicle, which could run primarily on methanol, but also could run perfectly normally on gasoline if you were out of range of the methanol station. That is actually what we took to production.

Working in industry, Dr. Nichols occasionally experienced times when her scientific judgment had to take a back seat to the realities of business.

Let's face it. Our bread-and-butter business in the auto industry is based on selling gasoline vehicles. Being a

Nichols saw her ideas go from research to production. She led the effort to design and produce this Ford Taurus, which was modified to run on methanol, ethanol, gasoline, or any combination of those fuels. "How many people in the auto industry can actually say they've ever had anything go to production? Not many!" she says with justifiable pride.

champion of alternative fuel vehicles was difficult sometimes. Even though I believed in that with my heart and
soul, there were times when I felt discouraged that more
people didn't understand this long-term need.

[Overall, however,] the periods of frustration were small
compared to the rewards of having achieved what I have.
How many people in the auto industry can actually say
they've ever had anything go to production? Not many! So
any time I feel discouraged, I can look at that and say,
"Gosh, you shouldn't feel discouraged; look at what you've
done!"

Over the course of a career, a scientist or engineer, especially in an industrial job, will almost surely encounter a situation in which corporate or political goals conflict with good
scientific or engineering practice. (See Chapter 7 for more detail on this issue.) When faced with such a situation, Dr. Nichols
takes a very practical approach.

First of all, you can't fool Mother Nature. If you're a
good scientist or engineer, the number one thing is adher-
ing to being objective and never compromising either your
project or yourself. It is absolutely appalling to me, for example, that occasionally you read about a scientist who has
"fudged" his data to make his results look better, or to make
things come out the way [he wanted, rather than what the
results indicated]. Eventually that will catch up with you.
So first and foremost, you must always adhere to the truth.
The truth is the most important thing.

And how does Dr. Nichols go about finding the truth when
it is so easy for people to mislead themselves under the pressure to produce a particular result?

If you can properly define the problem, you can find
the solution. It's the definition of the problem that is often
wrong, so people are searching for the wrong solution.

It's the ability to put pieces of the puzzle together. . . . The ability to think like that is the most important attribute for a successful scientist.

Dr. Nichols often speaks of the importance of leaving a legacy. From her work and her words, she will most likely be remembered as a practical environmentalist, for at the beginning of her interview and near the end, this is what she said:

The primary focus [of my work] has been [this question]: What will be the new energy sources for transportation use when we run out of petroleum? Even if it's 50 or 100 years away, it's a very difficult transition, so we've never felt it was too soon to start. . . .

I believe in change. A healthy system is a dynamic system. I have a master's degree in environmental engineering, and I get very frustrated when people talk in [negative] terms of "the environmentalists." I've asked the question after I've heard this phraseology repeated several times over and over. "What is an environmentalist?"

Well, an environmentalist is somebody who realizes the need to preserve Planet Earth as an ecosystem, but that doesn't mean that it has to remain unchanged. Change is a healthy part of preserving Planet Earth.

Some people would disagree with Dr. Nichols because they think that environmentalists stand in the way of progress and jobs. Others would disagree with her because she worked in the auto industry, and cars are polluting the air and destroying nature. How would she react to that? She would probably ask them if they have defined the problem correctly and then invite them to join her in searching scientifically for the truth.

Chapter Seven

Indira Nair: Ethics, Controversy and Living the Questions

My fervent and ardent desire,
Says gentle-voiced Indira Nair,
Is that adults and youth
Pursue wisdom and truth.
To integrity, all should aspire!

In novels and films, scientists are often portrayed as people so wrapped up in their work that they never consider the consequences of what they do. This stereotype arises because, without question, good scientists do find their work so compelling that they often become totally immersed in it. However, as the previous chapters illustrate, scientists are also real people with concerns that go beyond their laboratories and observations. They struggle, as do most people who find their work rewarding, to find a balance between work and the rest of their lives.

Indira Nair not only engages herself in that struggle, she also studies and teaches about that struggle in herself and others. As Associate Head of Carnegie Mellon University's Department of Engineering and Public Policy, she prepares scientists and engineers to deal with controversial issues, not by giving them answers, but rather by showing them the importance of raising and respecting the questions. She shows that to her students in the courses she teaches But more importantly, she shows everyone by example in the way she lives her life.

Indira Nair, Associate Head of Carnegie Mellon University's Department of Engineering and Public Policy, has gained the respect of colleagues on all sides of controversies where science, technology, and social issues come together.

Because I talk a lot about staying with the questions and listening to questions, rather than jumping to answers, one of my students sent me a poem by Riner Maria Rilke, who was a German poet, which starts, "Learn to love the questions." And it ends by saying, "Live the questions now, and perhaps someday you will live into the answers." As a scientist, perhaps that's how to begin: to live the questions.

Stay with the questions, Dr. Nair says, and listen to them. Those are two very important—and very different—aspects of being a scientist. Some scientists find a question to stay with early in life. Others move from question to question until they find one that "hooks" them. That was Dr. Nair's pattern.

It was probably fortunate that Dr. Nair's question-to-stay-with came to her—or she came to it—after she had worked as a scientist and taught science for more than 15 years. By that time, she had developed her skill of listening to and living the questions, not just asking them. She needed every bit of that skill, because the questions she asked led her to some very controversial issues and required her to face up to the limitations of the field in which she had earned her doctorate: physics.

Controversy arose over whether humans and other living organisms suffered any harm due to their exposure to very weak electric and magnetic fields caused by the everyday generation, transmission, and use of electricity. Epidemiologists—health professionals who study diseases that occur in unusually large numbers or clusters—saw evidence that some diseases, such as childhood leukemia, seemed to be correlated with living close to large electrical transmission lines.

The evidence was statistical, and no one could come up with a scientific theory of why the electromagnetic fields emitted by transmission lines, which were tiny compared to naturally occurring fields from other sources and in the body, could possibly have an effect. Could the reason for the effect be that the natural fields were more or less steady while the artificial fields oscillated (changed direction) roughly sixty times per second (a very low frequency compared to radio and other common electromagnetic waves)? Calculations by physicists, using a good mathematical model of the electromagnetic properties of living cellular material, indicated that any effect would be minuscule. The problem with those calculations, says Dr. Nair, is that the models treated the cell as just a hunk of material, not as something living.

This is how Dr. Nair describes her first encounter with the question, how she has stayed with it ever since, and how she has listened to it and lived it:

> It was almost accidental that I chanced into the issue that was first faced around 1978–79: the question whether low-frequency, low-intensity magnetic fields—at the time the question was electric and magnetic fields—have any impact on biological function, and therefore on health. [It was an important question,] because the use of electricity, which generates low-frequency magnetic fields, is ubiqui-

Electrical transmission lines such as these produce low-frequency electric and magnetic fields. Some health researchers believe that there is a correlation between a home's distance from transmission lines and its inhabitants' risk of developing certain forms of cancer and other health problems.

tous—or all over—in our society. Are we subjecting ourselves to some kind of low-level, eventual harm?

It was interesting as a scientific question. It was tantalizing to think about. It was also the kind of thing we did in the Department [of Engineering and Public Policy], which is why I chanced into it.

One of the areas in which we work is looking into how to decide, when the science is still uncertain [or] not done yet, what [the] health risks might be of [a particular] technology. [This question] fit [our departmental] profile; and as a social question, it suddenly became very important to me because I [realized] it was all pervasive, and it is obviously not some very radical effect. It's not overwhelmingly large; [otherwise,] we would have seen it by now. "Is there an effect?" was an emerging question as far as science was concerned . . . partly because [answering it requires discoveries in biology that] may be still to come.

This was a place where fundamental questions were being asked, [and] I had a chance personally to learn. I had to understand a lot of biology to understand [the] experiments [that] had been done. So in the learning, it was great. From the health-risk perspective, it was [something] new. The sociology of an emerging science was really neat. After I read papers and I went to a couple of meetings, I really got hooked, because of all these components: the societal aspect, technological aspect, and scientific aspect.

In the group that I worked with, there was no biologist, so I took it upon myself to be the person to understand and translate the biology. But I wasn't arrogant enough to think that I could learn in a few weeks—or a year, even—all the biology that one needed to know. I decided that what I needed to do was to talk to biologists frequently. In fact I would, as I talked to each person, ask them what elementary books I should be reading.

I learned a lot of the kinds of things that brought me to science [in the first place]. Then the question [for making government policy] is how [to] translate the emerging science into some decisions that [had to be made regarding] health risks of technologies already in our midst.

Dr. Nair's point here was that the technology—electric power generation—is a huge and very important industry in our society. Yet we are only now beginning to discover scientific evidence that it poses a previously unsuspected risk to human health. How does society decide how to balance the

INDIRA NAIR

Current field of work: Engineering and Public Policy

Business title and mailing address: Associate Head, Department of Engineering and Public Policy, Carnegie Mellon University, 5000 Forbes Avenue, Pittsburgh, PA 15213

Date and place of birth: July 31, 1940, Trivandrum, India

Education: B.S. (Physics and Mathematics), M.S., University of Bombay; M.S. (Physics), Kansas State University; Ph.D. (Physics), Northwestern University; Pennsylvania Teaching Certificate (Physics, Chemistry), University of Pittsburgh

Significant accomplishments:

- Review of biological effects of low-frequency magnetic fields for the United States Congress Office of Technological Assessment.
- Chair of Panel on Green Design (Design for the Environment) convened by the United States Congress Office of Technological Assessment.
- Co-founder, Carnegie Mellon University's summer Careers in Applied Science and Technology (CAST) program for high school students.
- Continuing to struggle to understand what makes for good teaching and good advising.

Previously worked as: Physics researcher (Bombay, India), high school teacher (Pittsburgh, PA)

Words of wisdom: If you're truthful—that means truthful with yourself and truthful with others, then you can say, "If I don't understand this, I can ask the question of either another person or the science. I don't have to pretend that I know the answer or that I am an expert." It's taking off your coping mechanism of the moment and trying to face things as they are.

risks with the benefits of the technology? Since many people have a financial or political incentive for making a particular decision, who should evaluate the evidence and how can the government determine a sound and appropriate policy?

She found herself, as a scientist, in an interesting position.

I had, perhaps, a unique position. . . . I was somebody who was educated in physics, [but] my feeling was, when I looked at the first experiments, that there was something there. Most of the physicists tended to disagree. Mine wasn't blind faith, but a lot of things made sense, [because] electric currents—electric signals—are used by the body for a lot of its functioning. So it made sense that electric and magnetic fields would influence the body.

Physicists forget that in biology there is one thing that hasn't been subsumed under physics, and that's life. In physics, we always treat a new thing the same way whether it's dead or alive. That's the crux of this [controversy] that's going on now.

A cell has internal structures that may react quite differently to an oscillating electric field, perhaps even a very weak one, than an inanimate object. Most physical models to date, however, leave out those structures in the analysis of the behavior of a cell in an electric field. Instead they treat the cell as if it is made of a single material and has the same electromagnetic properties throughout. Dr. Nair sees this as an opportunity to do some very interesting and new science.

I think it might be more than just a matter of doing more physics. We might have to do some different kind of physics. Maybe we'll have to think a little more strongly as to what is the role of time in biology. A lot of people have done a lot of work [there], but I think that area is where a lot of the crucial questions lie.

As she continues, Dr. Nair compares her excitement with the question with the experiences of young people who are just discovering the joys of science. She speaks of an inner voice that represents an individual's true self.

To find that kind of question, I was very lucky. If you are a young person trying to choose something, and you find a question that's *really* interesting then you think, "Oh, my God. Wow! It would really be nice to understand the elements of the question, if not the answer to the question." Then I think you should stick with it because it is really part of that inner voice advising you what your role in science might be.

Perhaps it catches your interest because it hooks on the right part of your brain, where you have this curiosity and this wonder. If a question intrigues you so much that it becomes part of you, and you catch yourself thinking of it at all kinds of times, then it is a clue to become engaged in that science.

It is said that Einstein asked his second-grade teacher what time is. The teacher was worried that he was a second-grader and he still couldn't understand time. But Einstein stuck with this instinct of wanting to know what time is, and it carried him much further than any teacher could have carried him. . . .

To each of us, there is a curiosity question. For me, this particular thing came very late in life, and I'm lucky that it came at all. But maybe, [for you, too,] there are questions that you won't let go.

A scientist is trained to be objective. A good scientist understands the scientific method not as a set of rules, but rather as a means to achieve intellectual honesty and objectivity. Following the scientific method, you may describe an idea as a *hypothesis*. However, when you have advocated an idea publicly and you have invested a great deal of effort and money in it, it is only human to resist or reject observations that contradict or weaken your position. Because of that, many observers of science—and many scientists as well—say that it often takes a generation for a revolutionary idea to gain acceptance, because the advocates of the old idea will actively oppose the new one until they retire or die.

Dr. Nair is a rarity among scientists. In the sometimes sharply divided community of scientists exploring the effects of low-frequency magnetic fields on humans and other living organisms, Dr. Nair is able to discuss and argue issues with nearly all the leading scientists on both sides. She has gained nearly universal respect in that area and in every other area in which she has worked because other scientists quickly recognize that she lives the questions instead of the answers. Her intellectual honesty and personal integrity shine through all of her actions.

How does a scientist—or anyone else—achieve that level of respect? For Dr. Nair, it is through the pursuit of three qualities.

> They're very closely related, yet they're not the same. One is authenticity. One is integrity. The other one is commitment.
>
> Authenticity is listening to yourself, meaning what you are as a person with respect to the science, for example. Then making sure that that inner voice gets to be part of this path to choose your decisions.
>
> Integrity means being true to yourself and true to the field you have chosen. Authenticity means discovering your true self; integrity is . . . action, . . . being able to exercise that trueness. . . . You have to be able to choose a place in life or choose avenues in life where you are able to exercise your authenticity, able to exercise your integrity.
>
> Integrity really has two parts. One part is keeping your pattern in life one whole, rather than being divided among so many things. . . . Integrity means a wholeness to what you do and what you pursue. But integrity also means one other thing that's really important. Going back to the origin of the word is integra, something that cannot be cut. . . . It has not only a wholeness in what you do, but it also has a core that is whole and steady, that cannot be cut. . . .
>
> That means that there is a part of you that is strongly with you, that is perhaps *not* compromisable. . . . In my ethics class, one of the things I tell my students to carry with them is the question "Are there one or two things so important to me in life that I will not compromise those?"
>
> Most of the values you hold, at some point or another,

under some conditions, may have to be traded away. So part of your authenticity is . . . being able to recognize when you trade them away, and being able to live with yourself for that.

But the integrity is identifying something that you cannot trade away. Also realizing that that is what makes you, and it's non-negotiable, no matter what an external validation tells you. It's something that gives you the core.

Commitment is being able to act on this. What I have had to learn the *very* hard way is that part of commitment means that there is a limit to the number of things you can commit to. . . . Commitment is recognizing what are the things you are absolutely committed to. Then realizing that as a person, you can only be committed to a limited number of things, and putting that restriction on yourself. Otherwise you won't be able to do the things that you want to do or the things you are committed to.

Closely associated with the idea of commitment is . . . a relatively new idea . . . called the ethic of care. If you are exercising an ethic of care, you'll know about the things you care about. You will work for those things or people, and you will work directly. For example, it's not part of an ethic of care if you send money to a charitable institution to do whatever it is you care about, [because] you are not there doing the caring action.

The other part of caring is caring in the dimension that the person or institution receiving the care requires—not what you think they ought to require. That means a real knowledge of the object [of your care].

Even with such a well-developed understanding of her own authenticity, integrity, and commitment, Dr. Nair still struggles with her own human limitations. For herself, and for young people who face the same struggle, she offers this advice.

My one rule or maxim for living is to try to be as truthful as possible. I find that the hardest thing for me is to be truthful with myself, because for survival, you can some-times put yourself into either a state of denial or a state of what would be untruthfulness if you looked at it really hard.

Truthfulness has helped me a lot in the sense of being able to do the work—do any work. If you're truthful—that means truthful with yourself and truthful with others—then you can say, "If I don't understand this, I can ask the question of either another person or the science. I don't have to pretend that I know the answer or pretend that I am an expert. I can ask the question." It's taking off your coping mechanism of the moment and trying to face things as they are.

Now Comes the Hard Part

You've heard from some people of science,
Including some often called giants.
Now comes the hard part.
Now your own questions start.
Da-DA-da, da-DA-da, da-DI-ence.

By now, the research project you began with the introduction to this book is well underway. Like any good research project, it has an open end, with lots of new questions for you to ask and pursue.

Now comes the hard part. Like the limerick at the beginning of this chapter, your research project is incomplete. It is up to you to consider many possible last lines that may tie the verse together. You may determine that you need to start from scratch with a different kind of poem altogether: the missing lines may fit into a different puzzle, and the final limerick may not match the rhythm or rhyme of your life.

You probably have been asking yourself lots of questions as you have been reading this book. If you haven't written those questions down, take the time to do so now. Think about what you liked about the scientists you met. Ask yourself how your life is similar to their early years. What have you done in the same way? What have you done differently?

What more can you learn about them and other scientists?

You may choose to re-read some of this book, or you may choose to find other data from other sources. People may suggest pathways to that new data, but you will probably discover the best, most rewarding trails on your own.

That's the hard part—and the fun, and it has just begun. Enjoy your research!

Glossary

This glossary will help you understand some of the important or more specialized scientific terms in this book. Those terms are italicized *like this* where they first appear in the main text and wherever they occur within this glossary. Some specialized words are not included here because they are fully defined where they are used and don't appear anywhere else in the book.

anamoly—a surprising, unexplained, or unexpected event or measurement, such as the unusually high concentration of iridium in the K-T boundary clay.

artifact—a human-made object (i.e. artificial, rather than natural). In anthropology and archaeology, the term is used to describe an object found at a "dig." An artifact can be as small as a fragment of pottery or a piece of a stone tool.

atom—the smallest unit of matter that can be identified as a particular chemical element. In this book, for example, Frank Asaro and Helen Michel (the scientists in Chapter 2) became famous because of their measurements of iridium atoms, and Richard Smalley (the scientist in Chapter 3) is known for his work with large molecules composed mainly or totally of carbon atoms.

barn—a unit that measures the "nuclear cross section" or the likelihood of a particular nuclear interaction, such as the capture of a neutron by a nucleus. The larger the cross section, the more likely the interaction. For example, an iridium nucleus has a relatively large neutron-capture cross section, which makes it possible to detect minuscule concentrations of iridium by neutron activation analysis.

chromosome—one of several sausage-shaped bodies within the nucleus of a living cell. Each chromosome carries certain genes and other life information encoded in DNA molecules.

clone—(verb) to create an identical cell or organism by genetic duplication of an original; (noun) a cell or organism created by cloning.

coma—the bright region surrounding the head of a comet. The coma is the comet's atmosphere, and it consists of dust and gases that have been driven off by radiant heat from the sun.

deoxyribonucleic acid (DNA)—a large molecule that contains the information that guides and controls the development and function of living organisms. It contains that organism's complete biological inheritance.

element—a substance that cannot be broken up into any other substances by a chemical process.

ethnobotanist—a scientist who studies the plant lore of a race or people.

forensics—the application of science in law; for example, the connection of an individual to a crime by matching parts of that person's DNA to the DNA in blood or other living cellular material found at the crime scene.

gamma ray—a packet of electromagnetic energy emitted by a radioactive nucleus as it decays. Each radioactive nucleus produces a gamma ray of a characteristic energy, the decay process has a characteristic half-life.

gene—a portion of a chromosome that carries a particular piece of genetic information. For instance, humans inherit their eye color from their parents through a pair of single genes, one from each parent.

gene splicing—cutting a piece of DNA from one chromosome and inserting it into another. This process makes recombinant DNA possible.

gene therapy—a method of medical treatment that attempts to repair or overcome a disease or other abnormal condition by delivering new genetic material into an individual's cells. The goal of treatment is new cells that function normally.

gene transfer—the transfer of a gene from one organism to another.

geomorphologist—a scientist who studies the relief features of Earth or other celestial bodies.

genetic map—a diagram that shows the set of markers along the chromosomes of an organism's genome.

genome—the basic arrangement of all genes on all chromosomes of a particular species. Each individual organism has a unique arrangement of genes, but all arrangements fit into an overall scheme that distinguishes that species from any other.

half-life—the length of time during which half of the radioactive nuclei of a particular kind undergo decay. Each decay gives off characteristic products (such as gamma rays of a particular energy) and has a characteristic half-life.

helix—a geometric structure that takes the form of a coil or spring. The DNA molecule exists as a double helix. It resembles a twisting ladder. The rungs of this ladder are nucleotide pairs.

human immunodeficiency virus (HIV)—the virus that causes the currently incurable and ultimately fatal disease known as AIDS, or Acquired Immune Deficiency Syndrome. In AIDS, HIV attacks and kills white blood cells known as T-lymphocytes or T-cells that play an important role in the immune system. When the T-cells die, they burst and spew out fresh HIV to attack uninfected cells. Eventually, the infected individual has very little defense against infectious diseases and certain types of cancer.

human genome—the genome of the human species. The Human Genome Research program seeks to map the human genome and to identify the variations that are possible within it.

hypothesis—a tentative assumption that is tested during an experiment or observation.

iridium—a very dense metallic element. The discovery of unusually high concentrations of iridium in a layer of clay at the K-T boundary suggested that the clay was formed as a result of an impact by a massive body from outer space. This led to a major change in our understanding of the causes of mass extinctions as seen in Earth's geologic history.

inherit—to receive genetic traits from a parent during reproduction.

K-T boundary—The geologic layer that marks the end of the

Cretaceous period and the beginning of the Tertiary period of Earth's history, about 65 million years ago. Below this layer, the fossil record shows many species of plants and animals, including dinosaurs, that seem to have rapidly died out in a mass extinction.

map—in the context of genetic research, the noun *map* means a detailed diagram of the arrangement of nucleotides on the DNA of a particular organism; the verb *to map* means to make such a diagram.

marker—an easily identifiable region along a chromosome, which serves as a reference point for making a genetic map. The position of each gene on that chromosome is identified by making reference to a set of more-or-less evenly spaced markers.

matter—anything that occupies space and has mass. The universe consists of matter and energy, and the science of physics deals primarily with the many forms of those two entities and the relationship between them.

mitosis—a process in which a living cell divides into two cells, each identical to the original cell.

molecule—the smallest unit of matter that can be identified as a particular chemical compound. A molecule consists of two or more atoms bound together in a particular way. For example, a water molecule is made up of two hydrogen atoms attached to one oxygen atom; a buckminsterfullerene molecule is made up of sixty carbon atoms bound together in the shape of a soccer ball; a protein molecule can be made up of thousands of atoms.

neutron—one of the basic building blocks of an atom. An atomic nucleus consists of a cluster of neutrons and protons. If a neutron strikes a nucleus, it may be captured and the result may be a radioactive nucleus that will, after some time, give off a gamma ray. In that case, neutron activation analysis can be used to determine the relative concentration of each type of nucleus in a sample of material.

neutron activation analysis—an important technique in chemistry that enables the detection and identification of minute concentrations of particular elements. In this technique, a beam of neutrons strikes a sample of material. The nuclei of some of the atoms in the sample absorb neutrons, become radioactive, and decay. As a nucleus decays, it gives off gamma rays of a characteristic energy and a characteristic half-life. By measuring the intensity of gamma rays as a function of time, scientists can determine the concentration of the various atoms that produced them.

nucleotide—one of four basic chemical units [adenine (A), thymine (T), cytosine (C), and guanine (G)] that, when paired with its complementary nucleotide (A with T and C with G), forms the rungs of the ladder on the DNA double helix.

nucleus (plural *nuclei*)—the central part of an atom, which carries most of its mass, and is made up of protons and neutrons. (When referring to a living cell, the nucleus is the central part of the cell, which contains the DNA.)

physical map—a diagram of a genome that enables a scientist to locate a specific gene precisely on a particular chromosome by counting the number of nucleotide base pairs between that gene and a marker.

predispose—to create a tendency for a certain condition or situation to occur. For example, the inheritance of a specific gene may predispose a person to a particular illness, but the person may nevertheless have the good fortune not to develop that illness.

protein—a large molecule that carries out a particular function in a living organism. The organism's DNA contains the instructions for how and under what conditions to make thousands of different proteins.

recombinant DNA—artificial DNA molecules made by splitting other DNA molecules and recombining the pieces in a different pattern from the original. In this way, a gene from one species can be spliced into another. Recombinant DNA has been used to make bacteria that produce valuable human proteins, such as insulin, human growth hormone, and human blood clotting factors. A bacterial culture can sometimes be used to produce these substances in large quantities while avoiding the serious risks, such as allergic reactions or dangerous viral infections, that may be associated with such proteins produced from human or animal sources.

severe combined immune deficiency (SCID)—an inherited condition in which the individual lacks the ability to fight off infections. One famous SCID patient, known as David, the Bubble Boy, lived in a plastic bubble that protected him from infection. He died when an experimental treatment failed and he was exposed to normally harmless bacteria in the environment. Today, SCID patients are treated with a wide variety of medical regimens, including gene therapy.

shocked quartz—a form of the mineral quartz that has been subjected to a great deal of pressure, such as might be caused by a powerful nuclear explosion or the impact of a massive body from space. Its crystal structure shows defects, such as normally parallel atomic layers that have been fractured.

stem cell—the cell in the bone marrow from which all blood cells are derived. Since HIV seems to be unable to reach and infect stem cells, scientists are attempting to treat infected individuals with stem cell gene therapy.

subduction—literally, being drawn under. According to the well-established geological theory of plate tectonics, the Earth's crust is made up of several plates that slowly move past one another. Where they come together, the edge of one plate is subducted beneath the other.

synthetic—produced artificially by combining substances or components.

T-lymphocytes (T-cells)—one type of white blood cell (see *human immunodeficiency virus*).

Additional Information

- A number of colleges, universities, and other organizations offer summer science programs for young people. One of the best places to start looking is the *Directory of Student Science Training Programs*, published periodically by Science Service, Inc. 1719 N Street, N.W., Washington, D.C. 20036.

- A major source of funding for student science experiences is The Directorate for Education and Human Resources, National Science Foundation, 4201 Wilson Blvd., Arlington, VA 22230. The Directorate provides support for a variety of summer and year-round programs run by colleges and universities for junior high school and high school students.

- The National Science Foundation also supports University "Centers of Excellence," which include some programs geared toward high school students. You can get a list of the Centers and their research areas by writing to the Engineering Research Centers Program (if your interest is primarily engineering) or the Science and Technology Centers Program (if your interest is primarily science) at the National Science Foundation, 4201 Wilson Blvd., Arlington, VA 22230.

- Do an on-line computer search. If you don't have a computer in your home, your school or public library may have one. On the World Wide Web, you can find many home pages and sites for government organizations, such as the National Science Foundation(http://www.nsf. gov/) and the National Institutes of Health (http://www.nih.gov/), and for professional societies, such as the American Association for Advancement of Science (http://www.aaas.org/). You may also find on-line discussion groups on many interesting topics.

Index

Italics indicate illustrations.

About the Author

After completing his Ph.D. in theoretical and computational physics at Carnegie Mellon University, Fred Bortz taught college physics and mathematics and did research in computational physics. He also worked on space-related projects for two summers, nuclear reactor design for 3 years, and automobile engine control systems for 3 years. Dr. Bortz then returned to Carnegie Mellon, where he worked for 15 years on microprocessor applications, advanced computer disk systems, engineering design, and science education. He also spent 2 years on the faculty of the Duquesne University School of Education.

Dr. Bortz has published three books for young readers—*Superstuff! Materials that Have Changed Our Lives*; *Mind Tools: The Science of Artificial Intelligence*; and *Catastrophe! Great Engineering Failure and Success,* which was designated a Selector's Choice on the National Science Teachers Association-Children's Book Council list of Outstanding Science Trade Books for Children for 1996. He also founded the National Forum on Children's Science Books and co-founded Careers in Applied Science and Technology, a 6-week summer program for high school students.

Dr. Bortz lives in Monroeville, PA, with his wife Susan, who works as a tutor and as a program and administrative consultant. They have two grown children—Brian, who teaches science in an elementary school, and Rosalie, who is exploring her own path toward a career in research.